This
Summer
Robbie Orbie

For all the lovers of Summer

Evelyn Waugh

"If it could only be like this always—always summer, always
alone, the fruit always ripe."

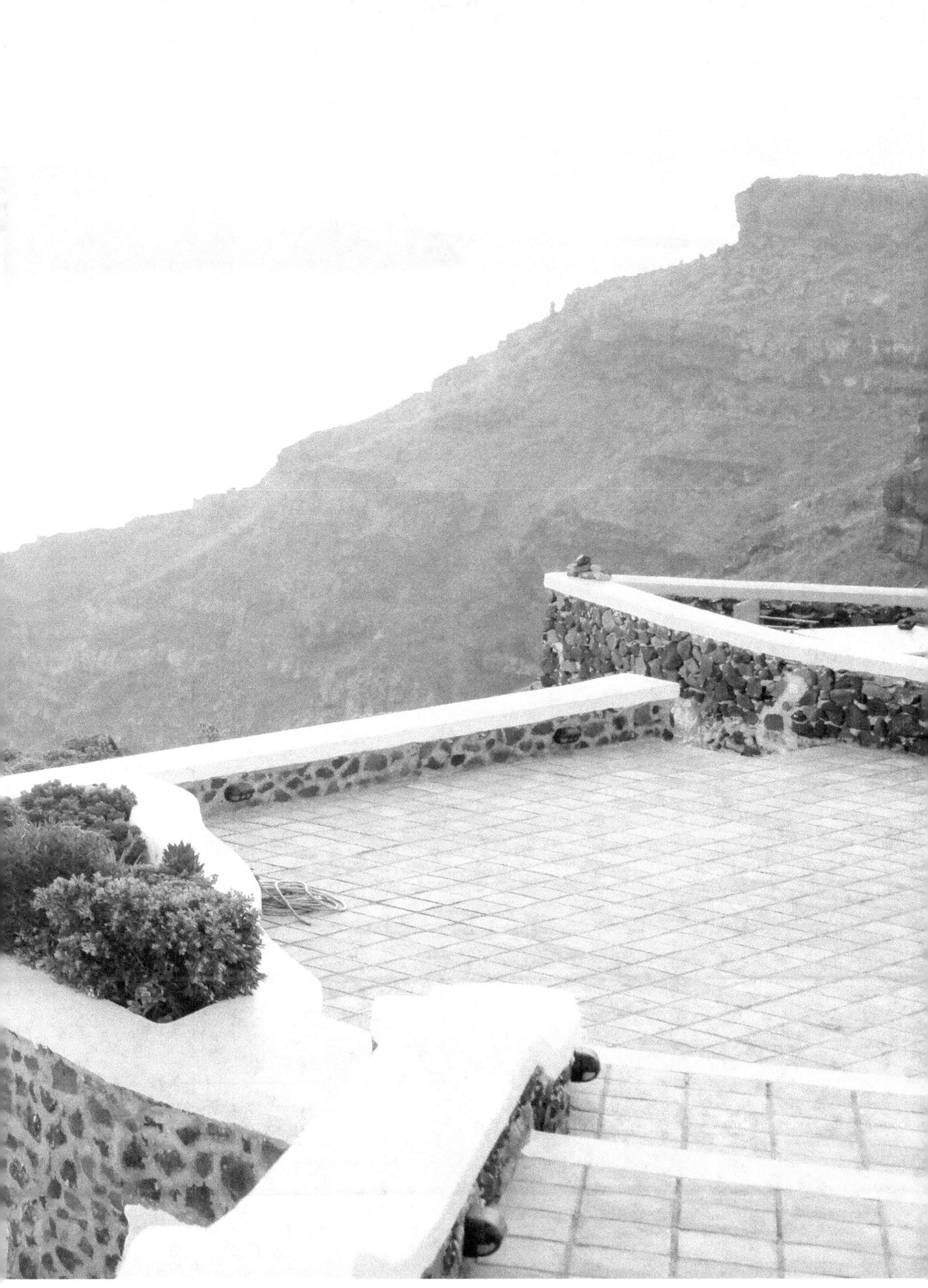

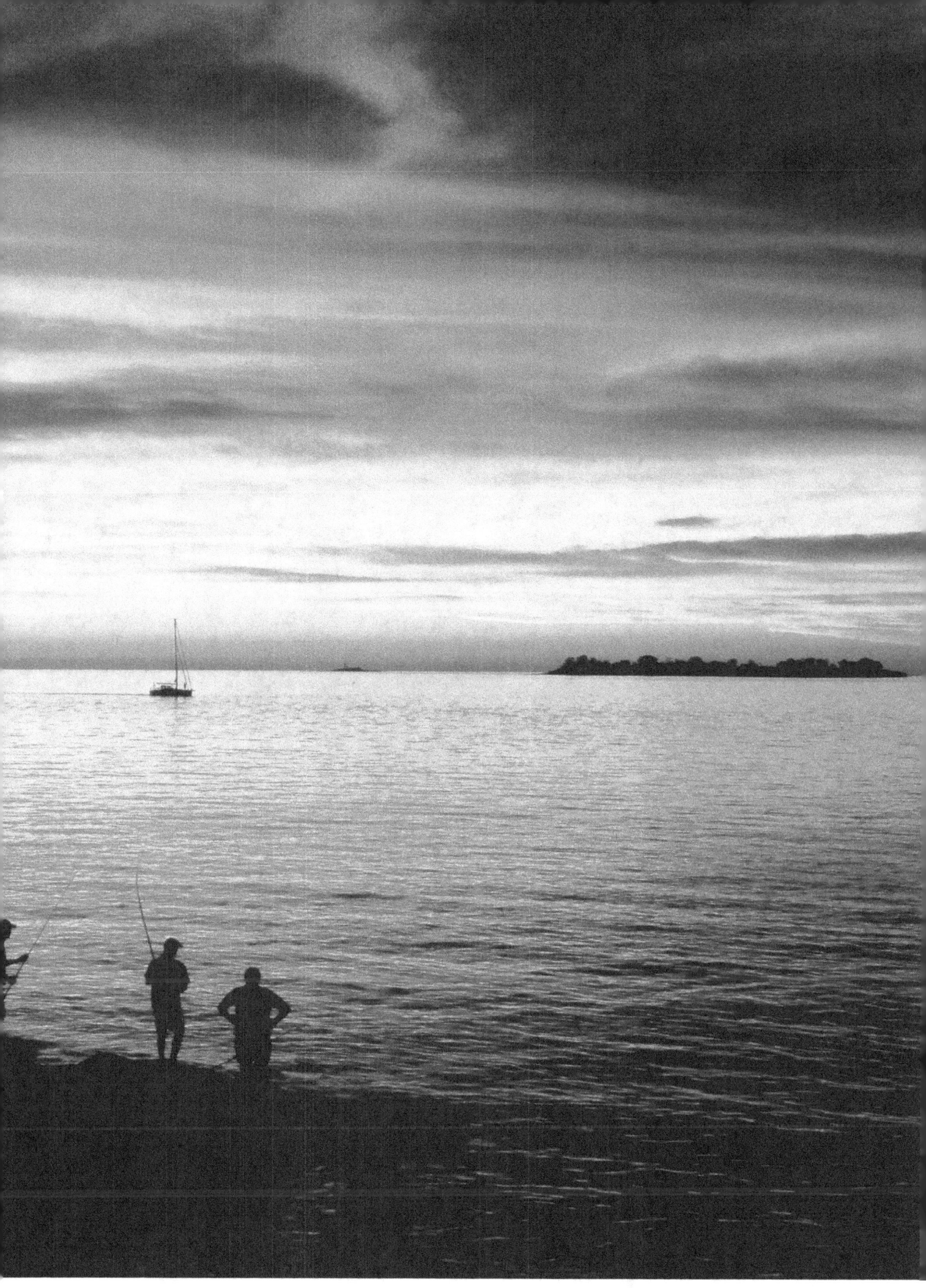

C. Day Lewis
"Summer has filled her veins with light
and her heart is washed with noon."

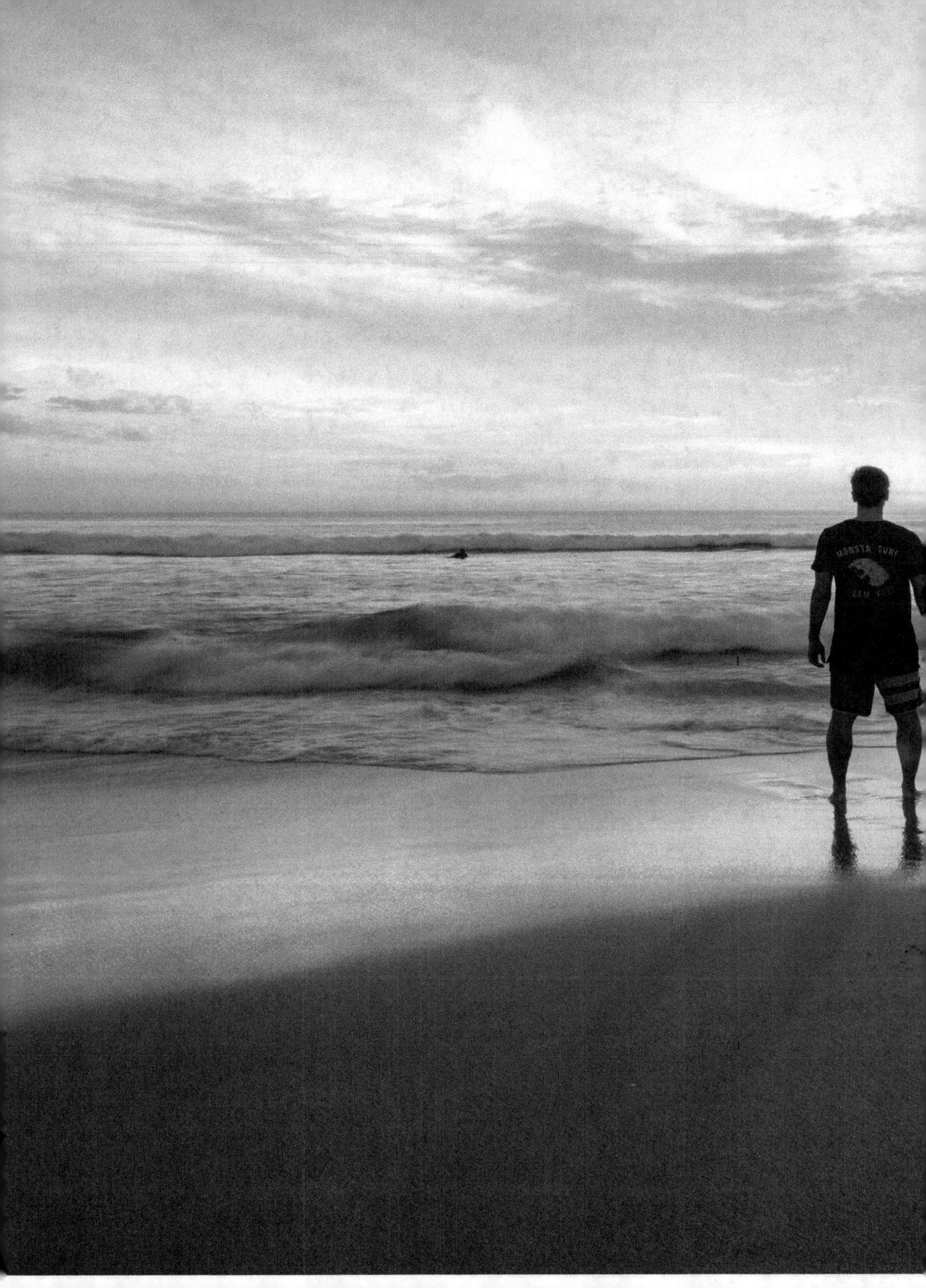

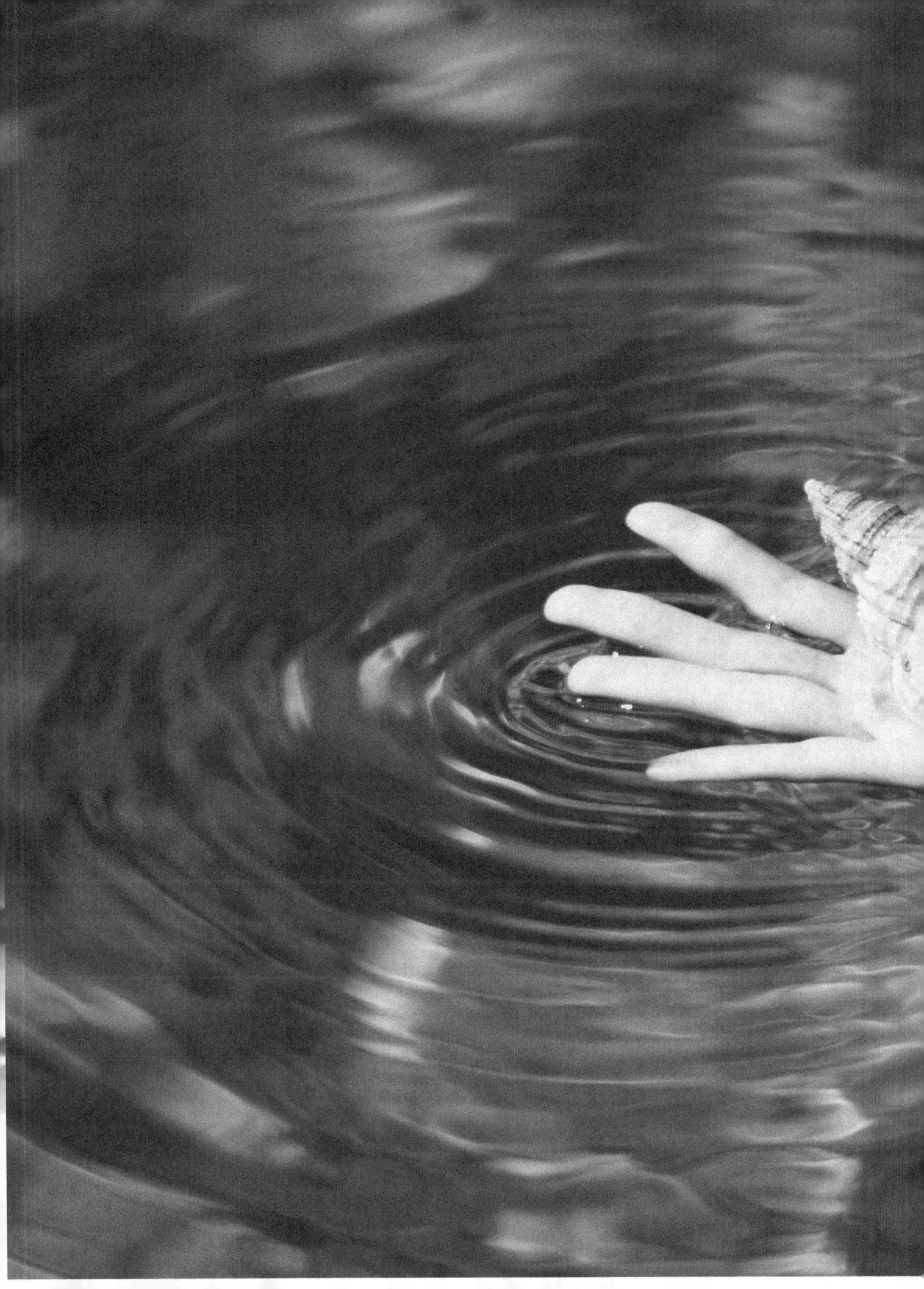

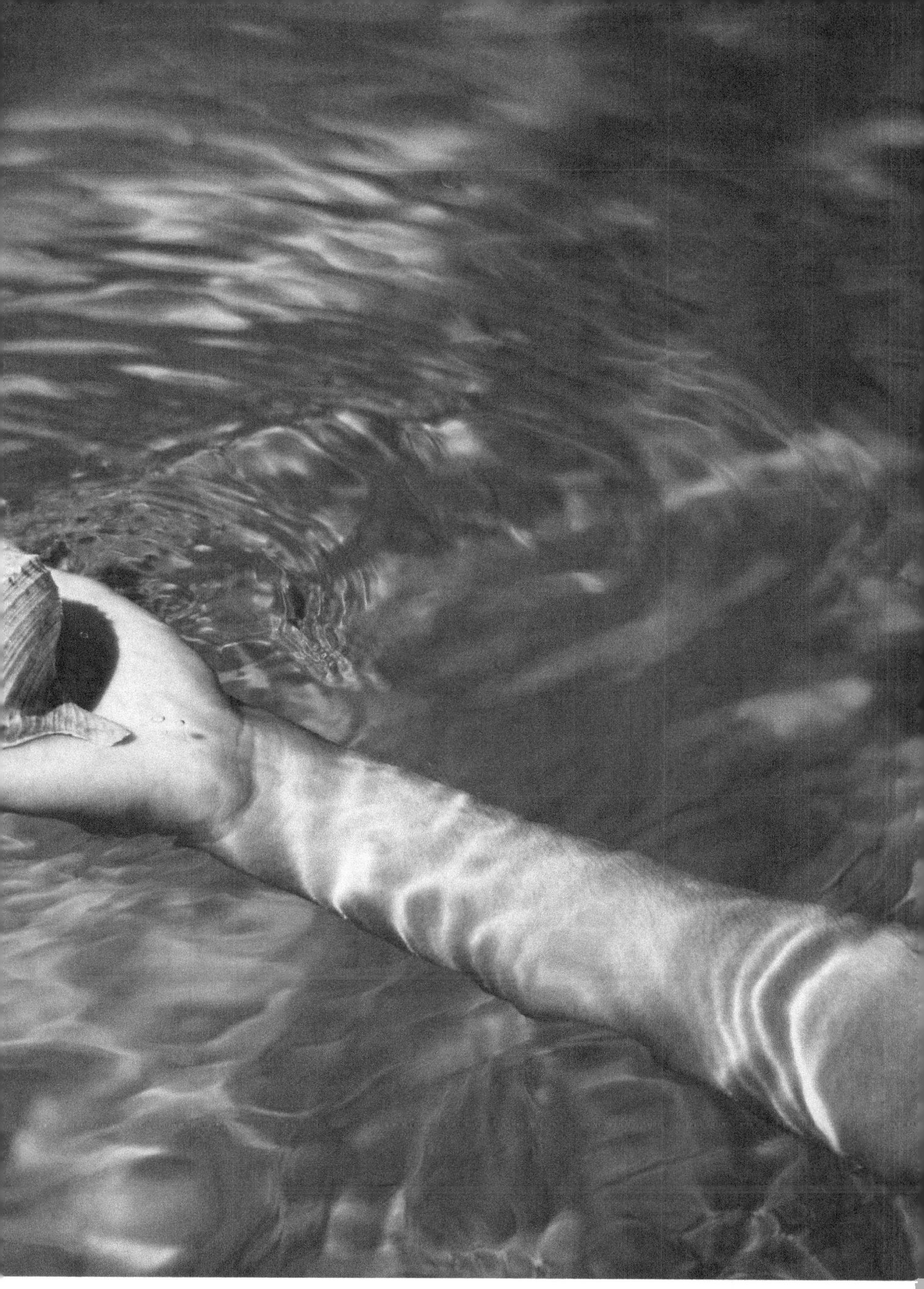

Henry David Thoreau
"One must maintain a little bit of summer, even in the middle of winter."

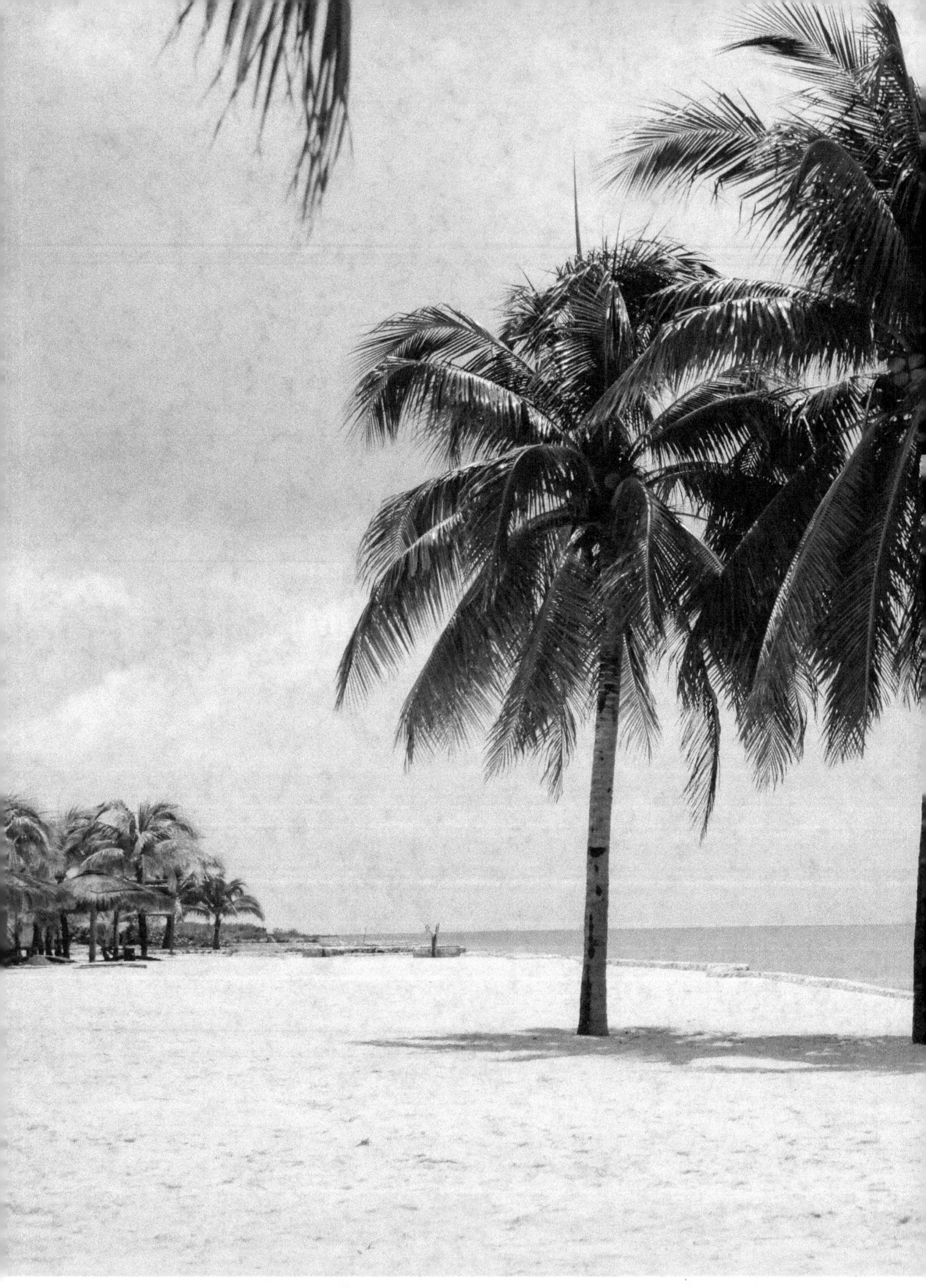

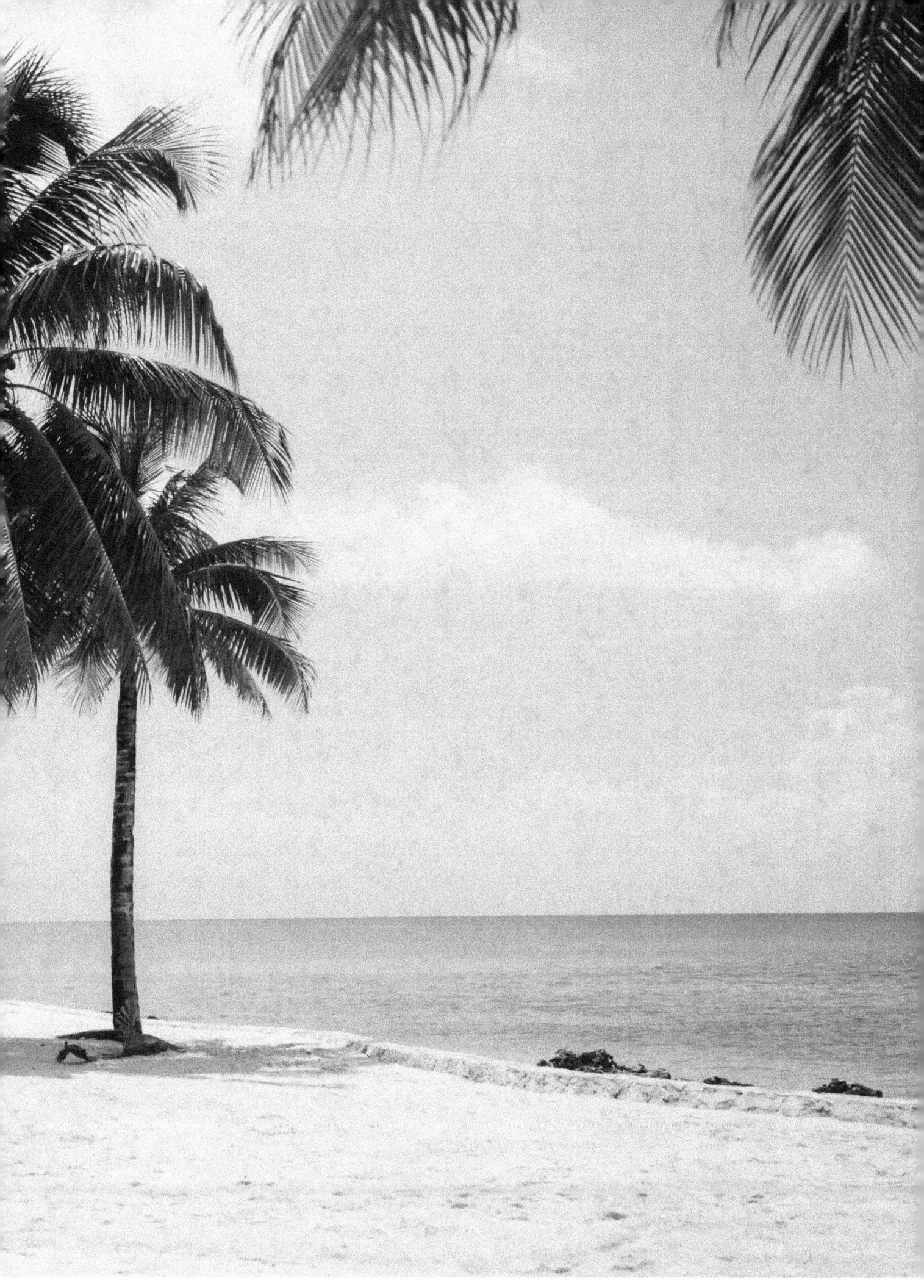

Katie Lee
"If summer had one defining scent, it'd definitely be the smell of barbecue."

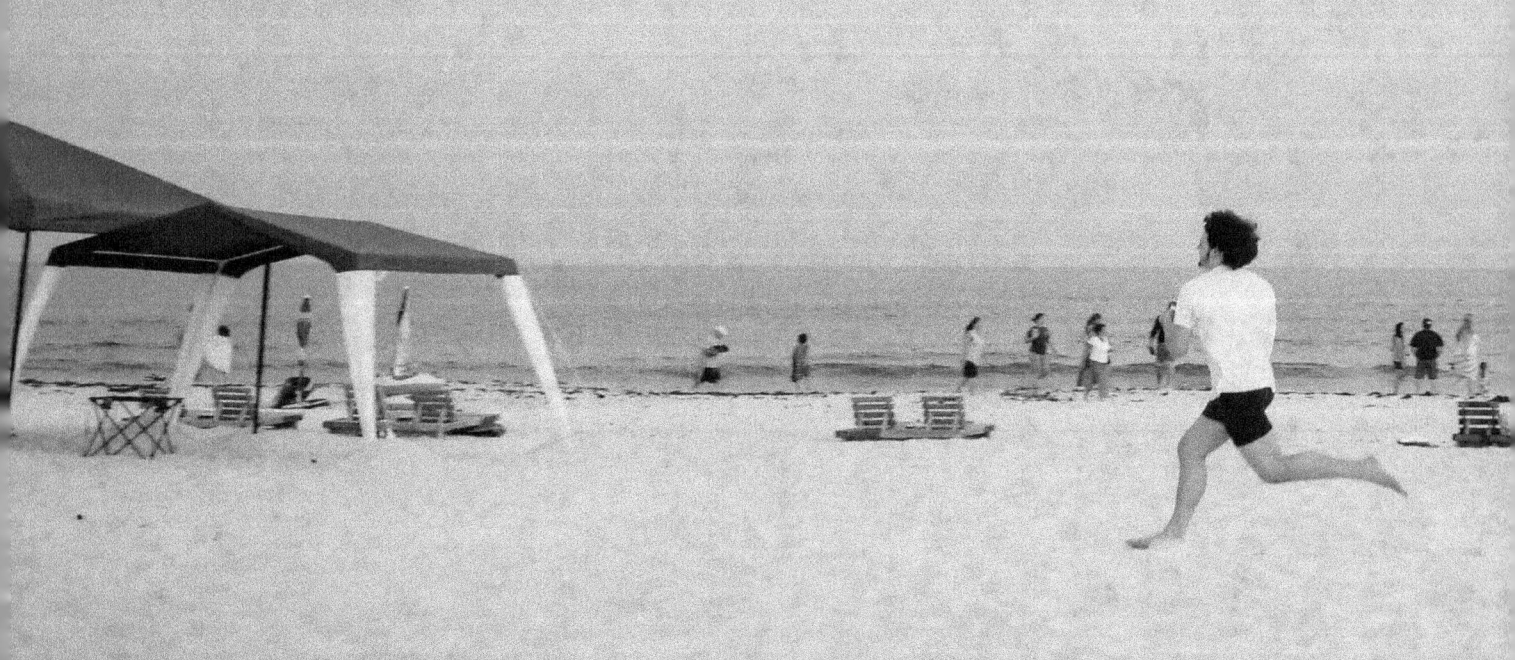

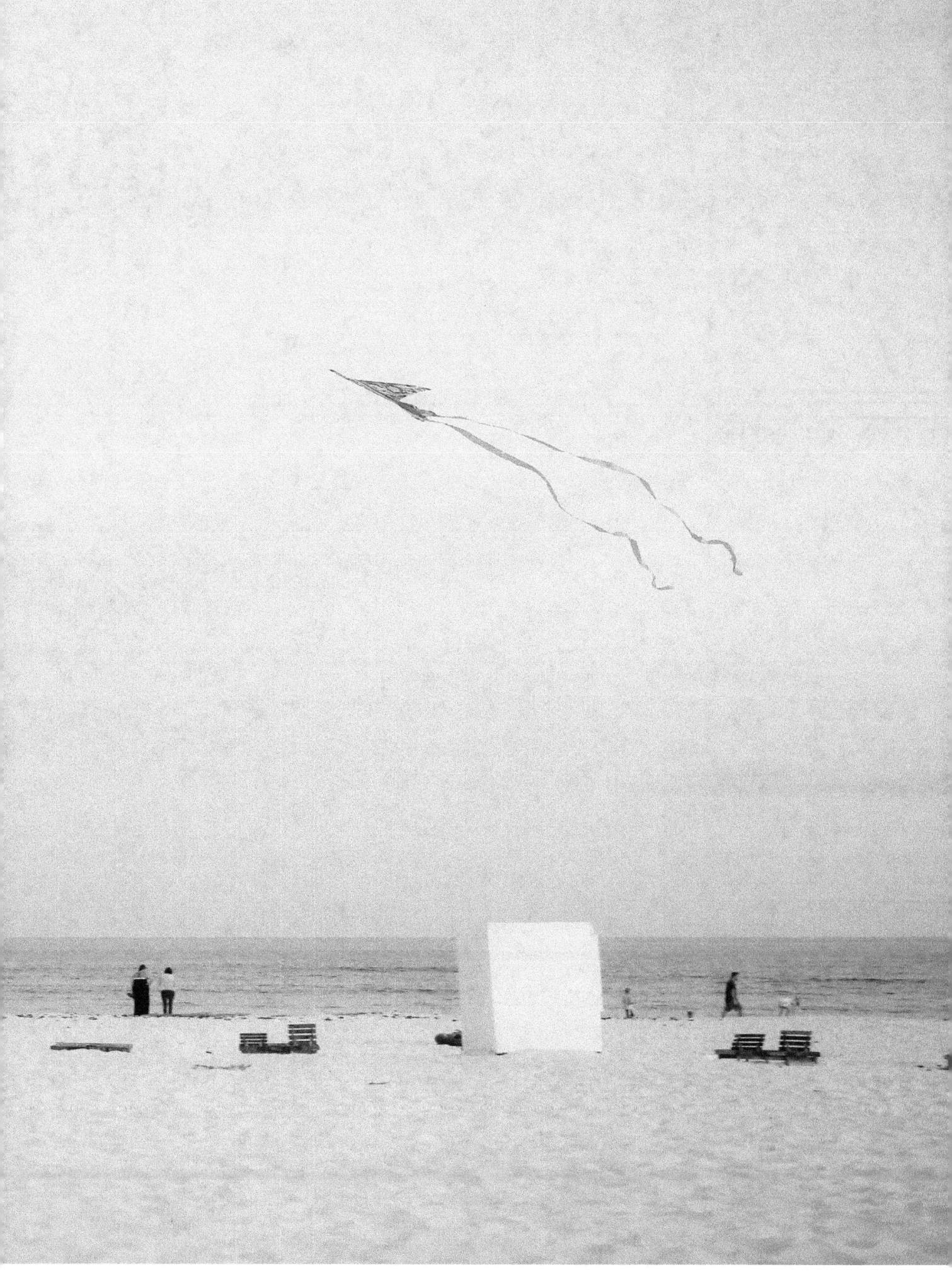

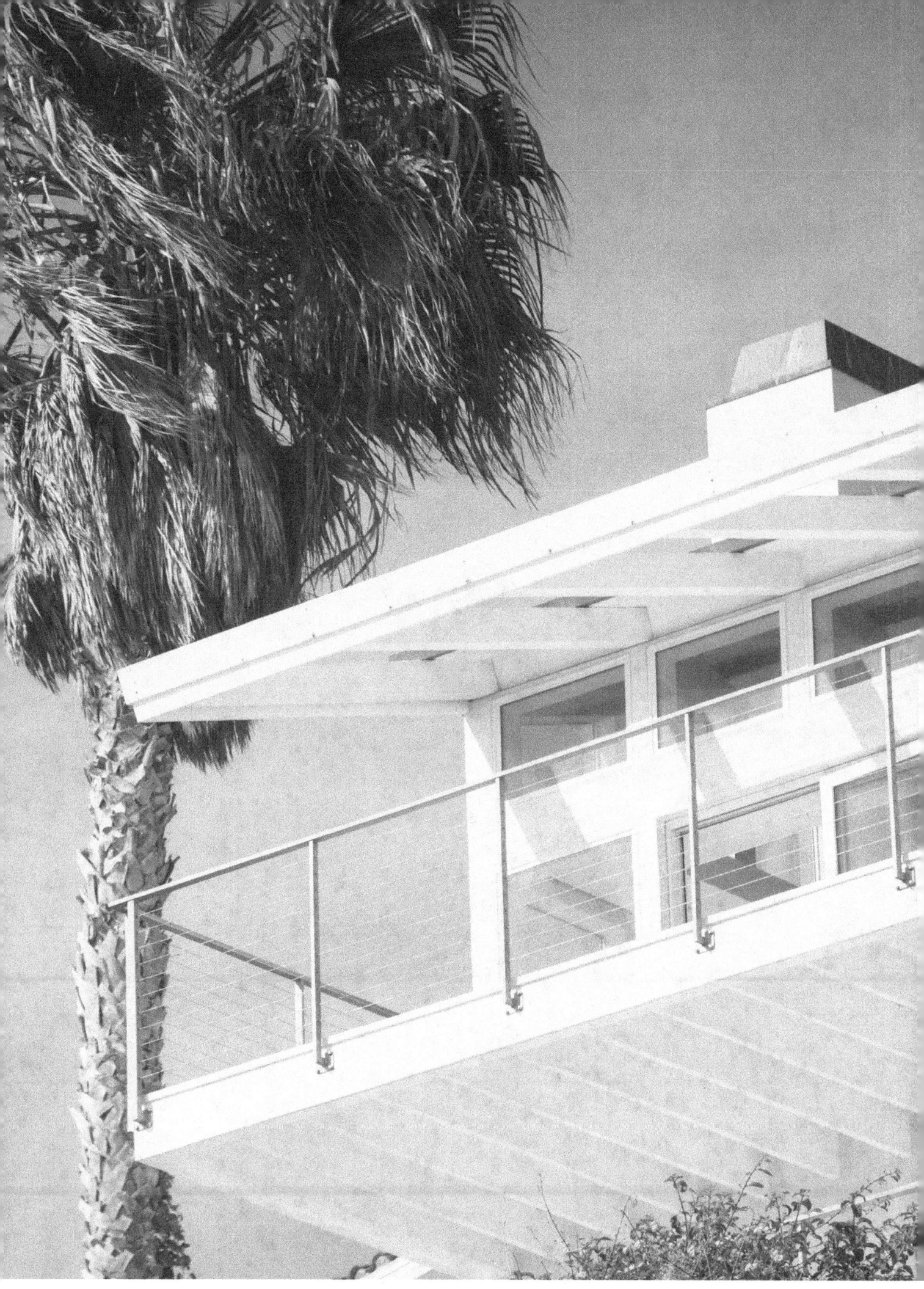

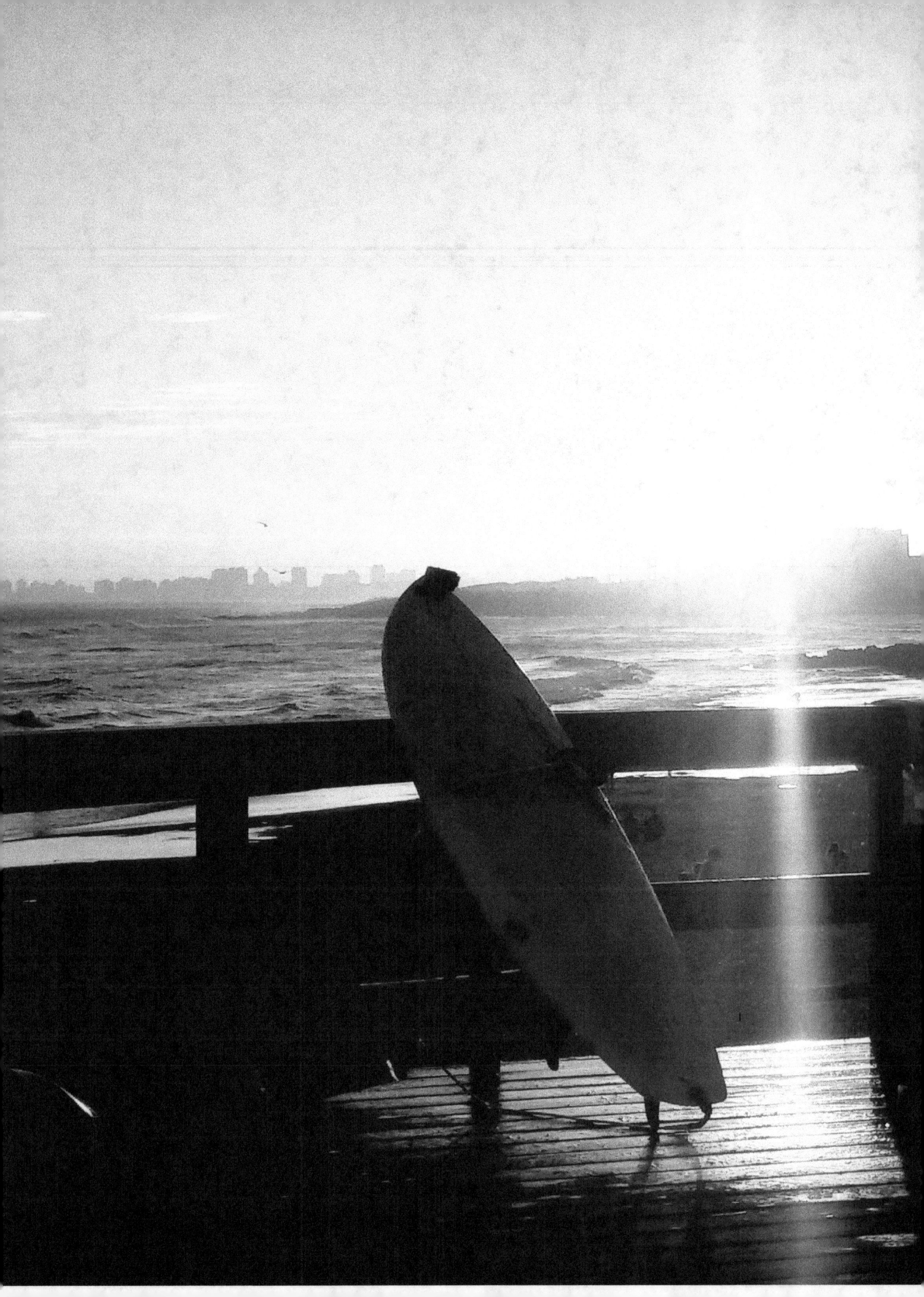

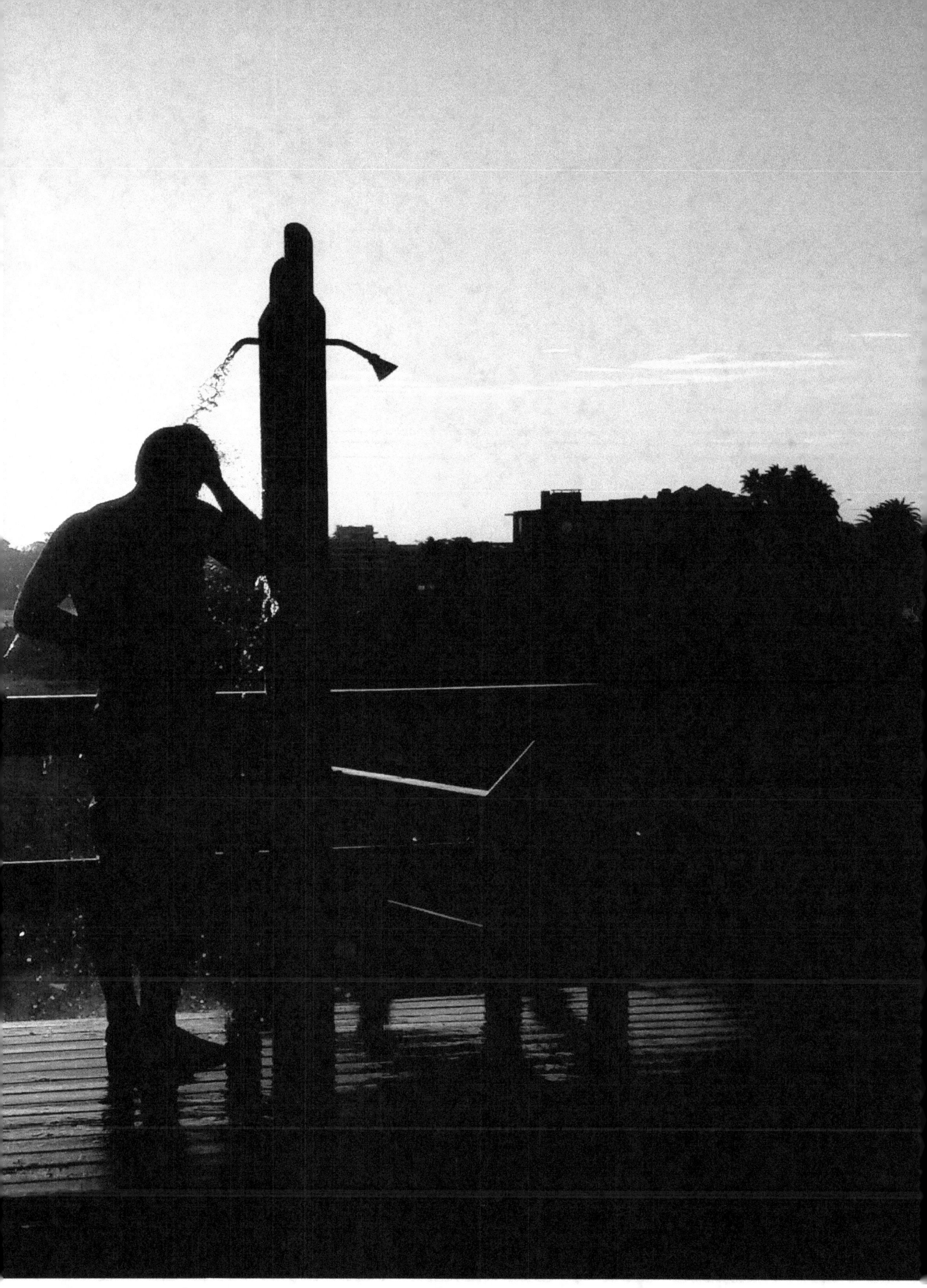

Al Bernstein
"Spring being a tough act to follow,
God created June."

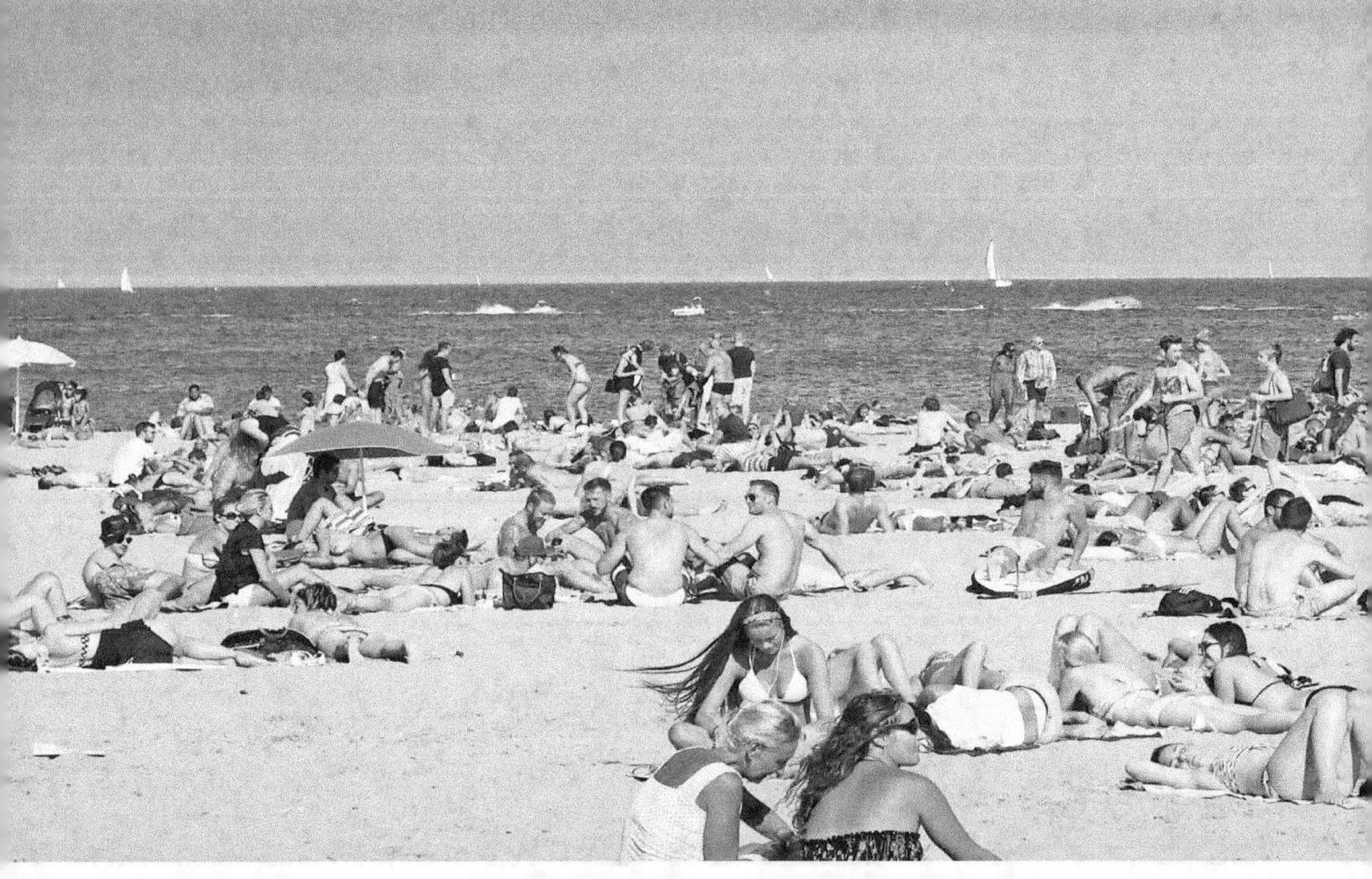

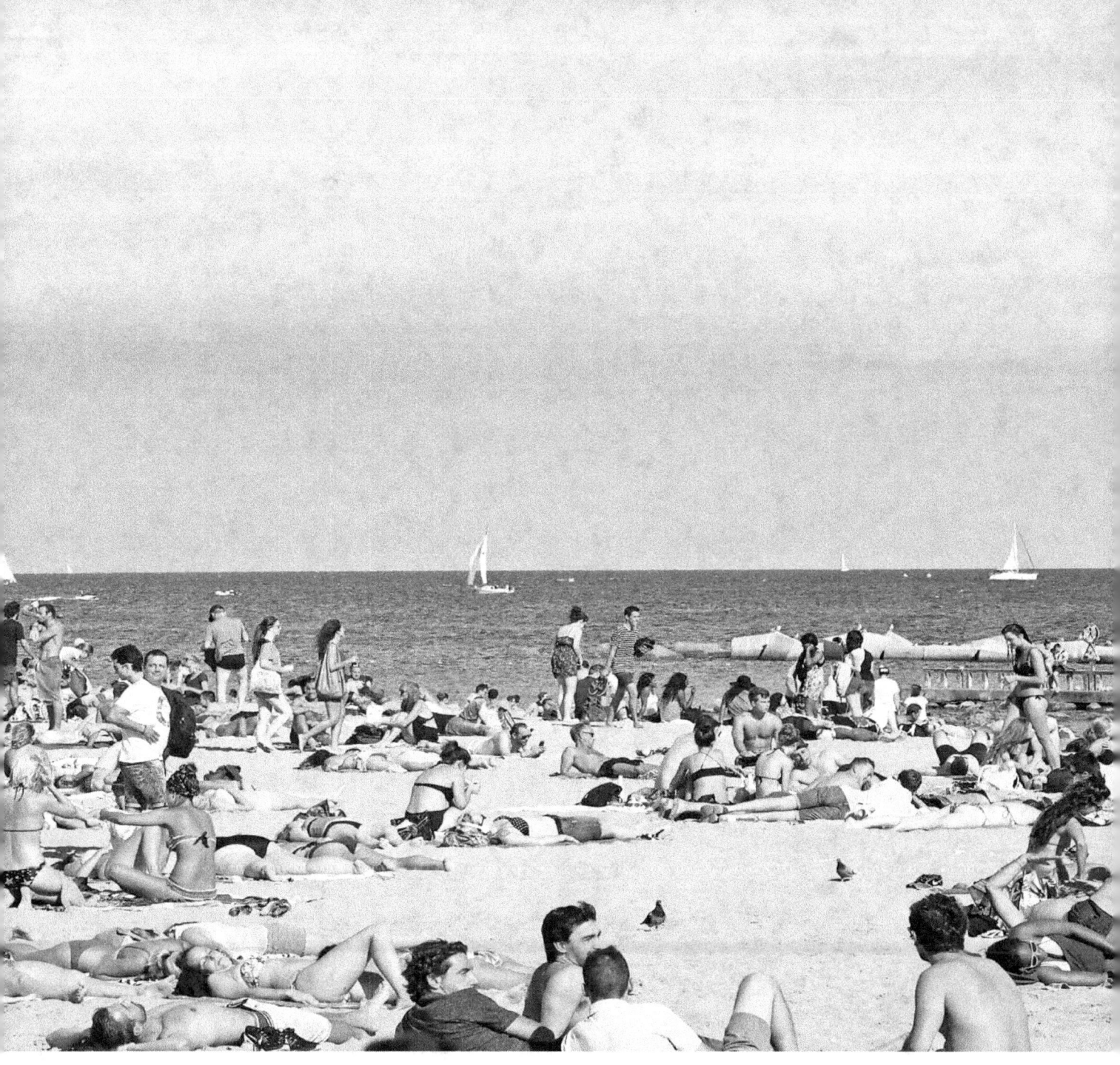

Jack McBrayer
"I love summertime more than any-
thing else in the world. That is the only
thing that gets me through the winter,
knowing that summer is going to be
there."

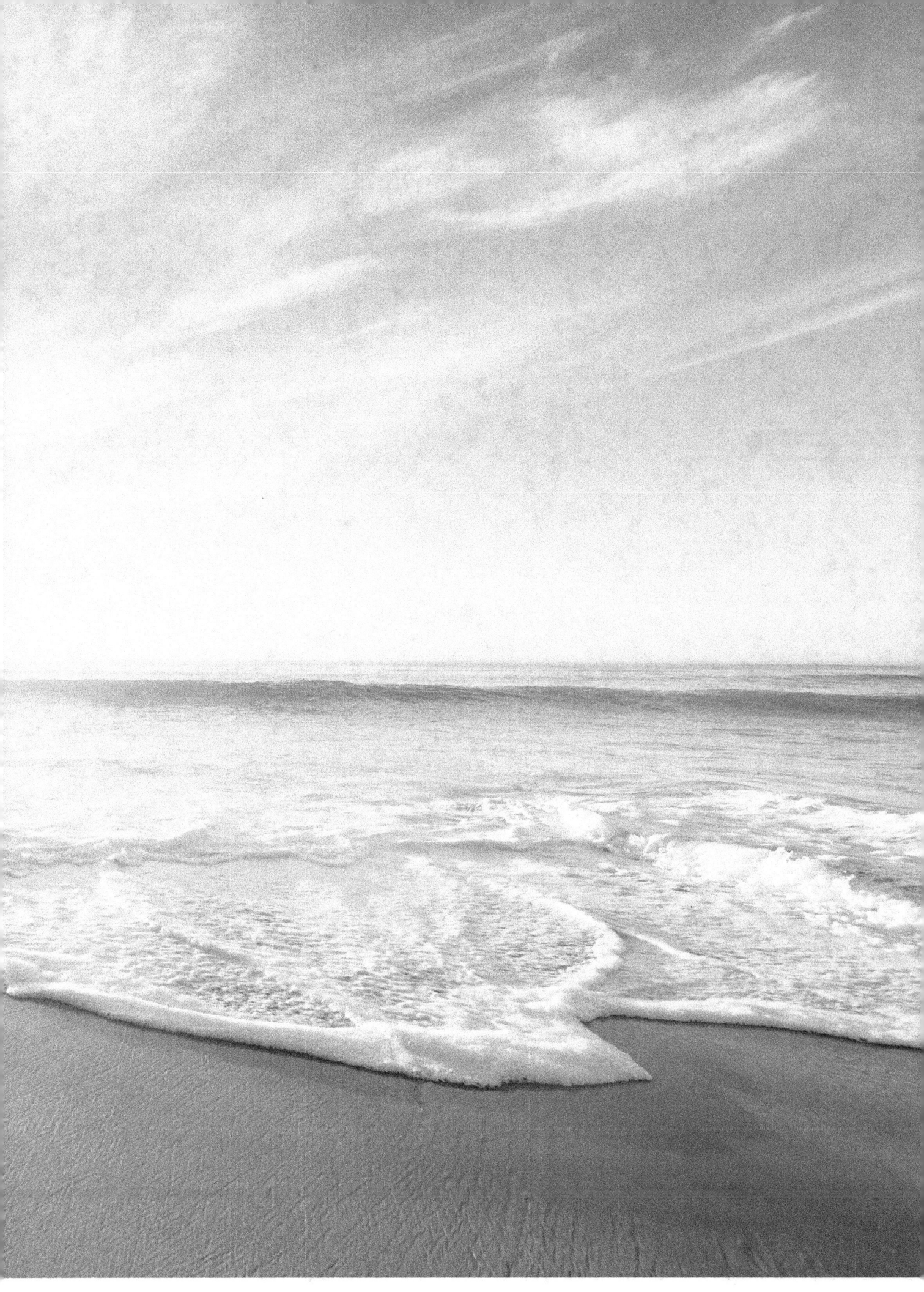

Audrey Hepburn
"To plant a garden is to believe
in tomorrow."

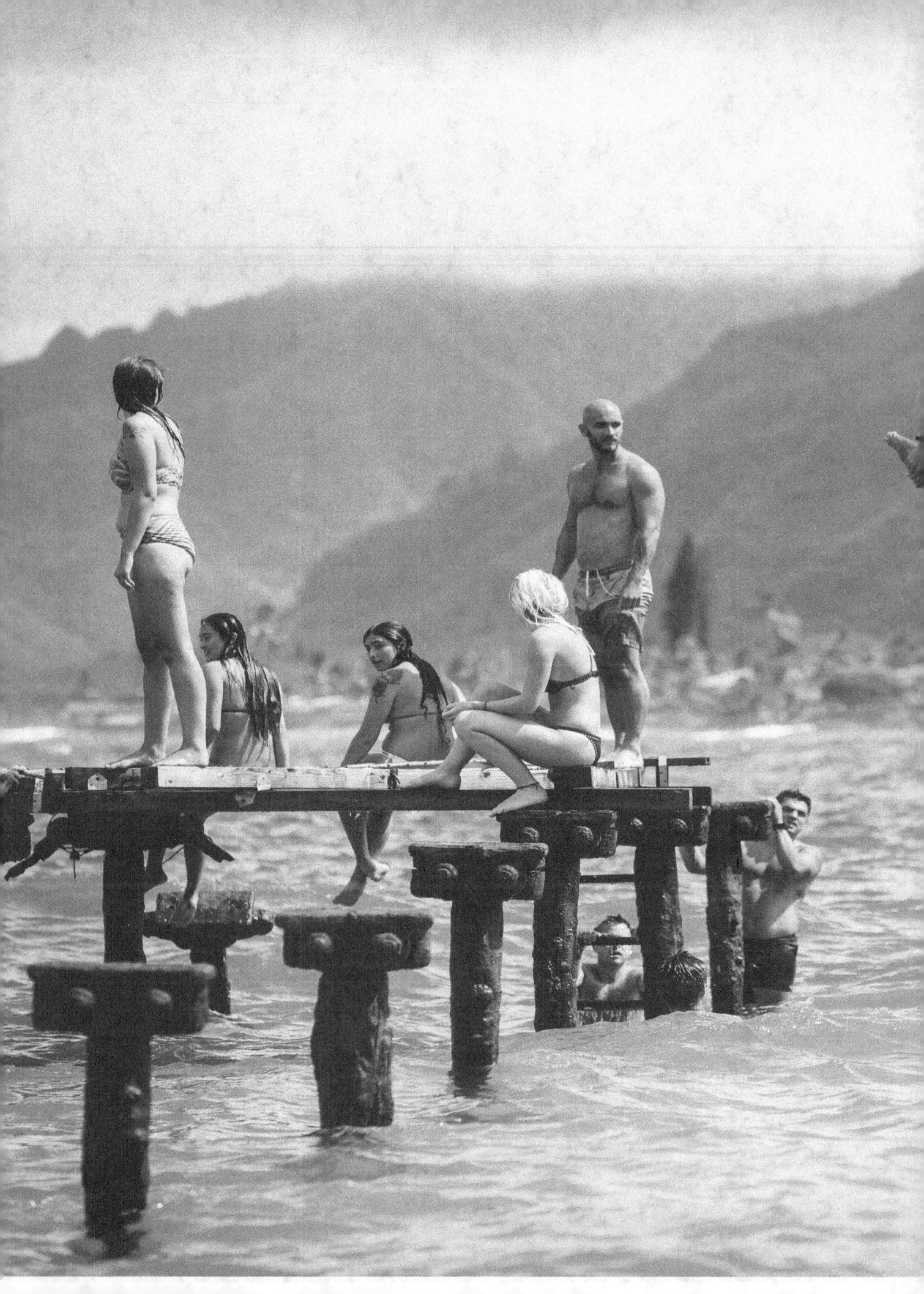

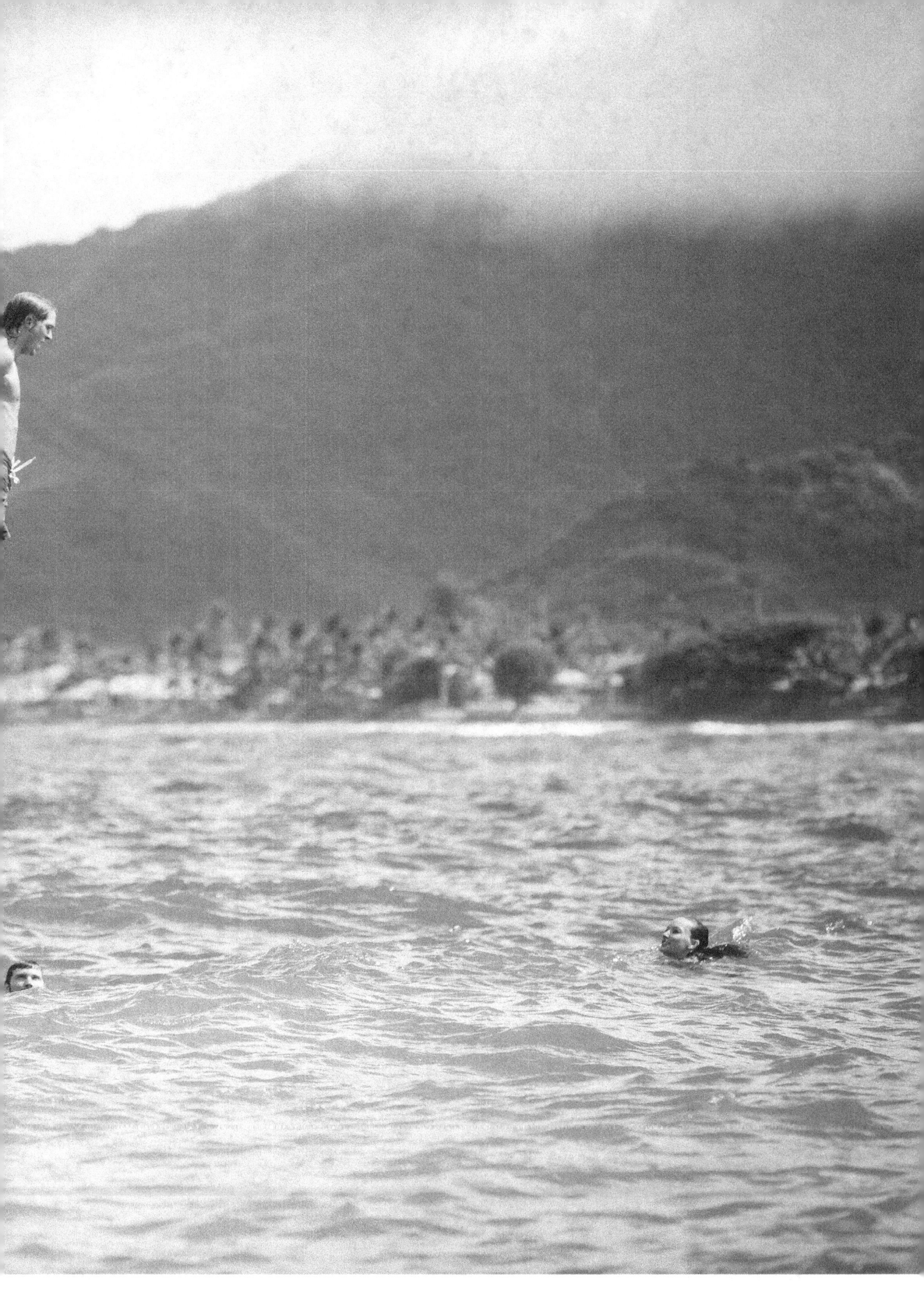

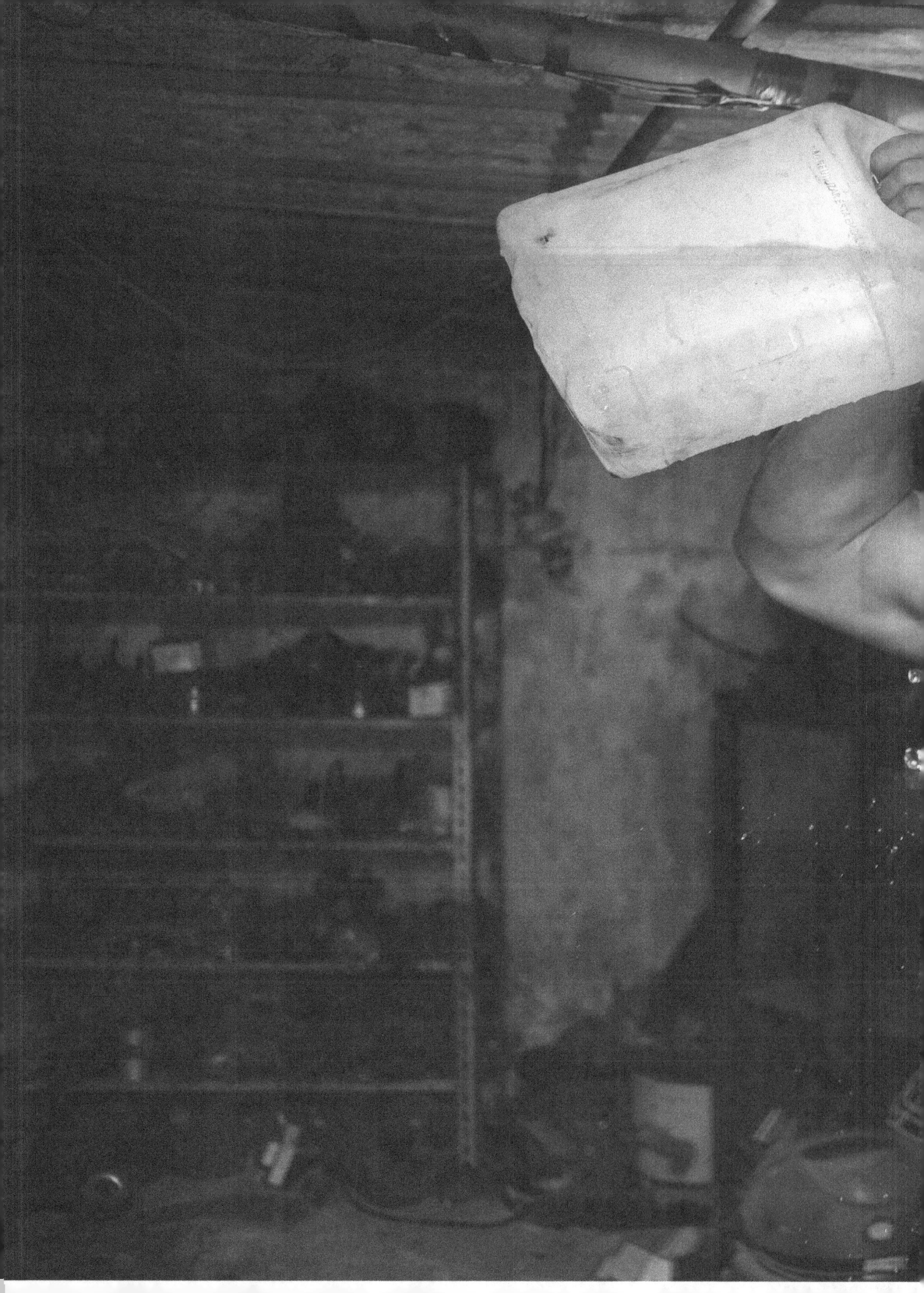

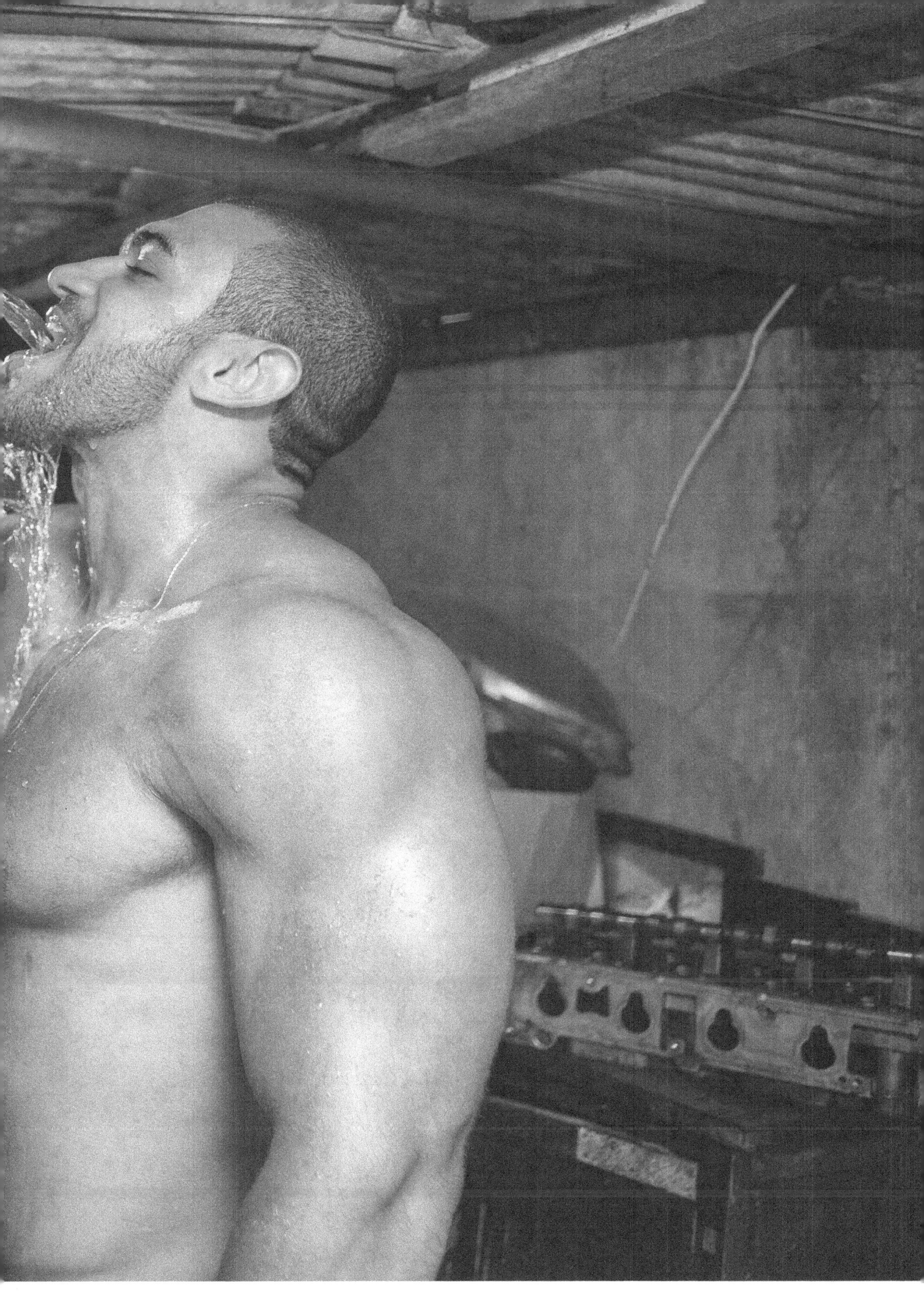

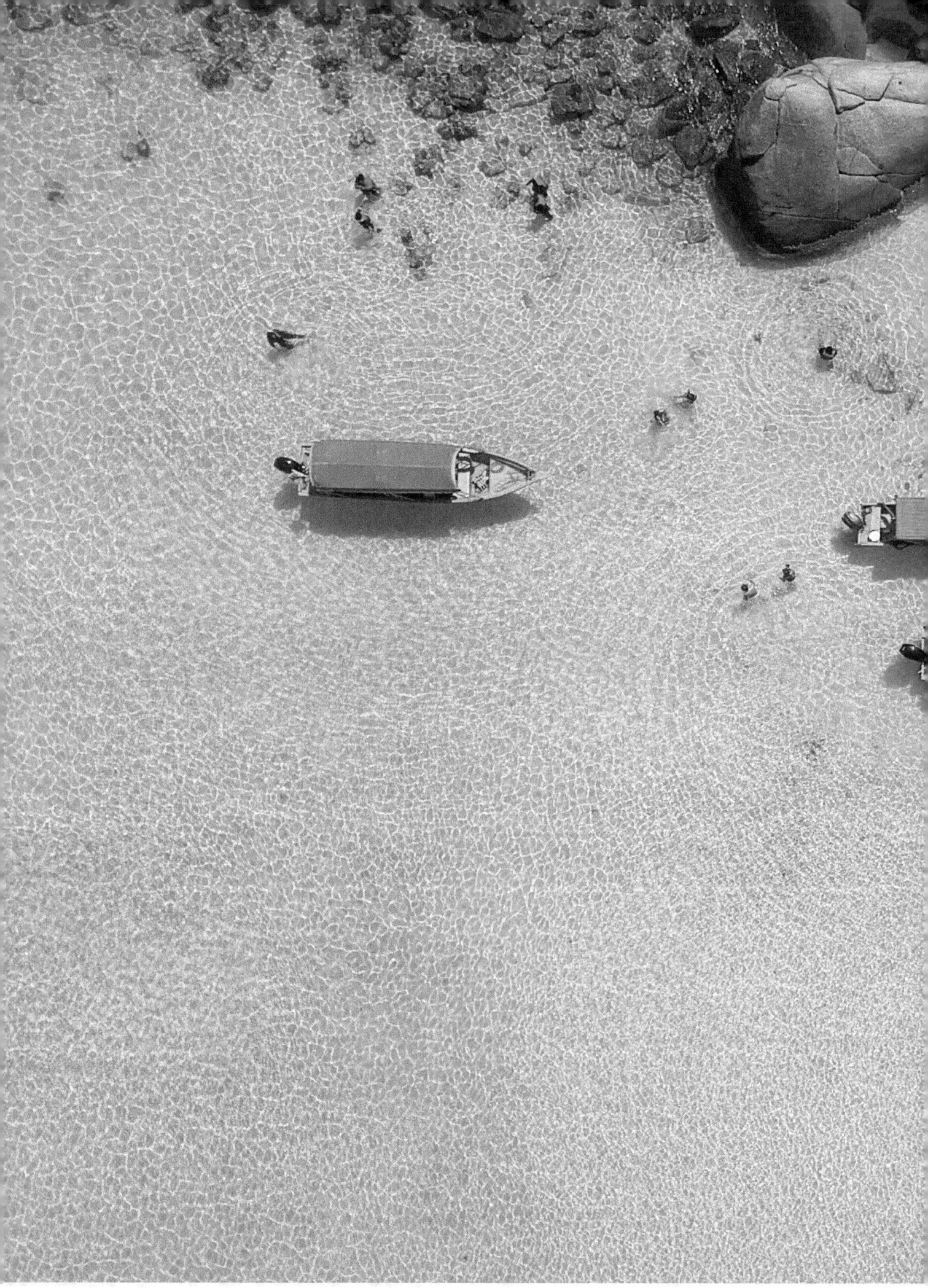

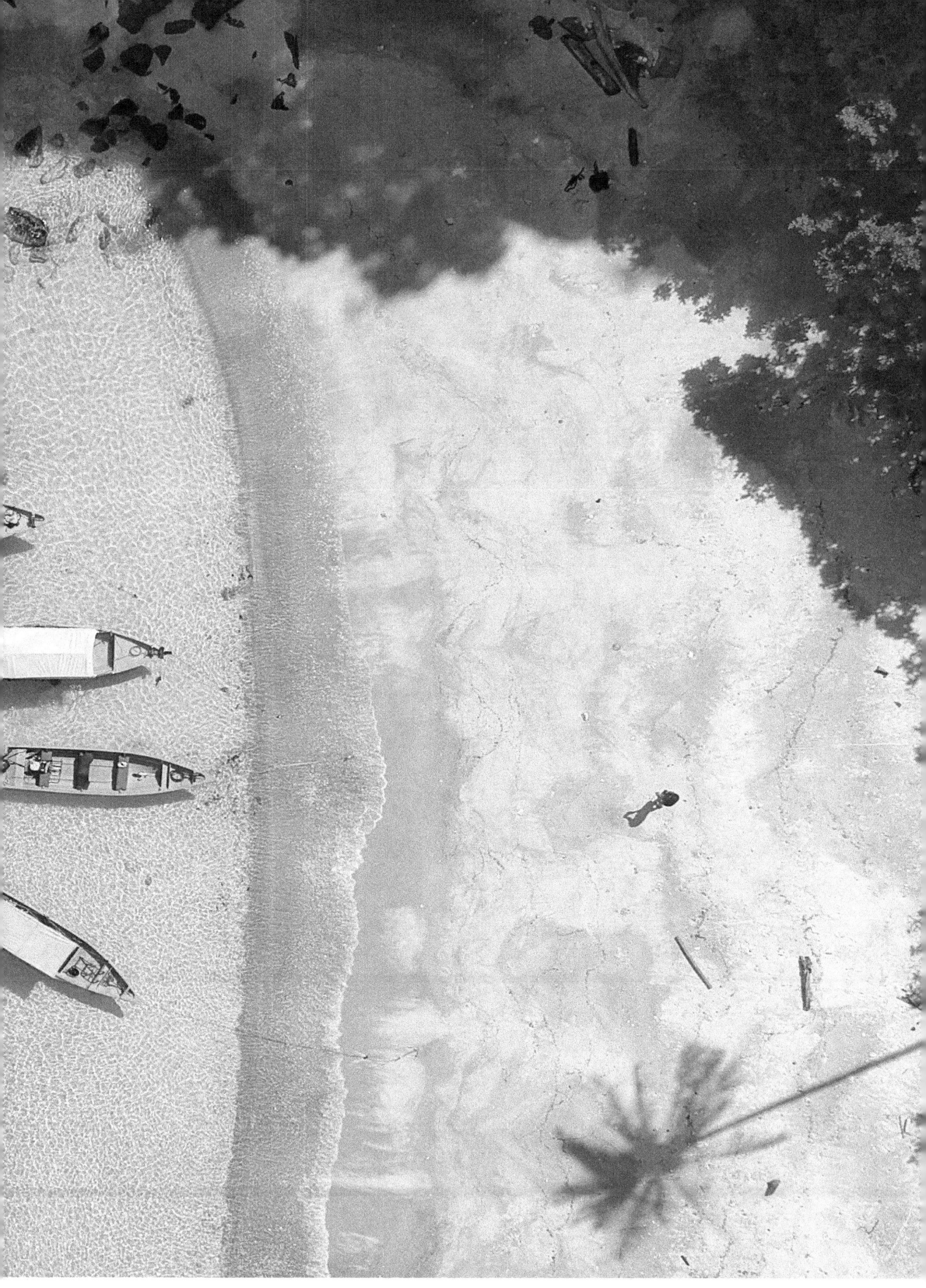

Charles Bowden
"Summertime is always the
best of what might be."

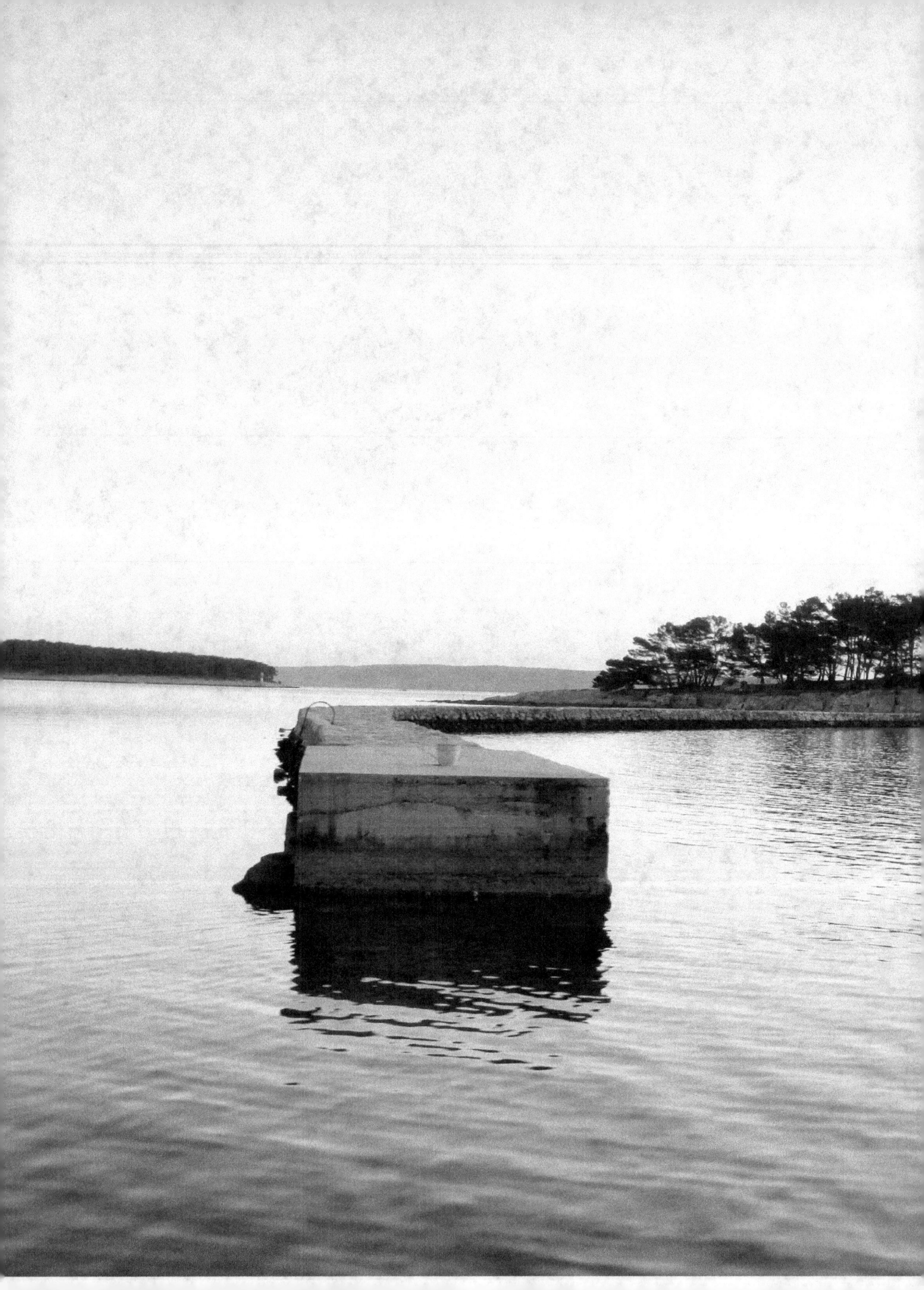

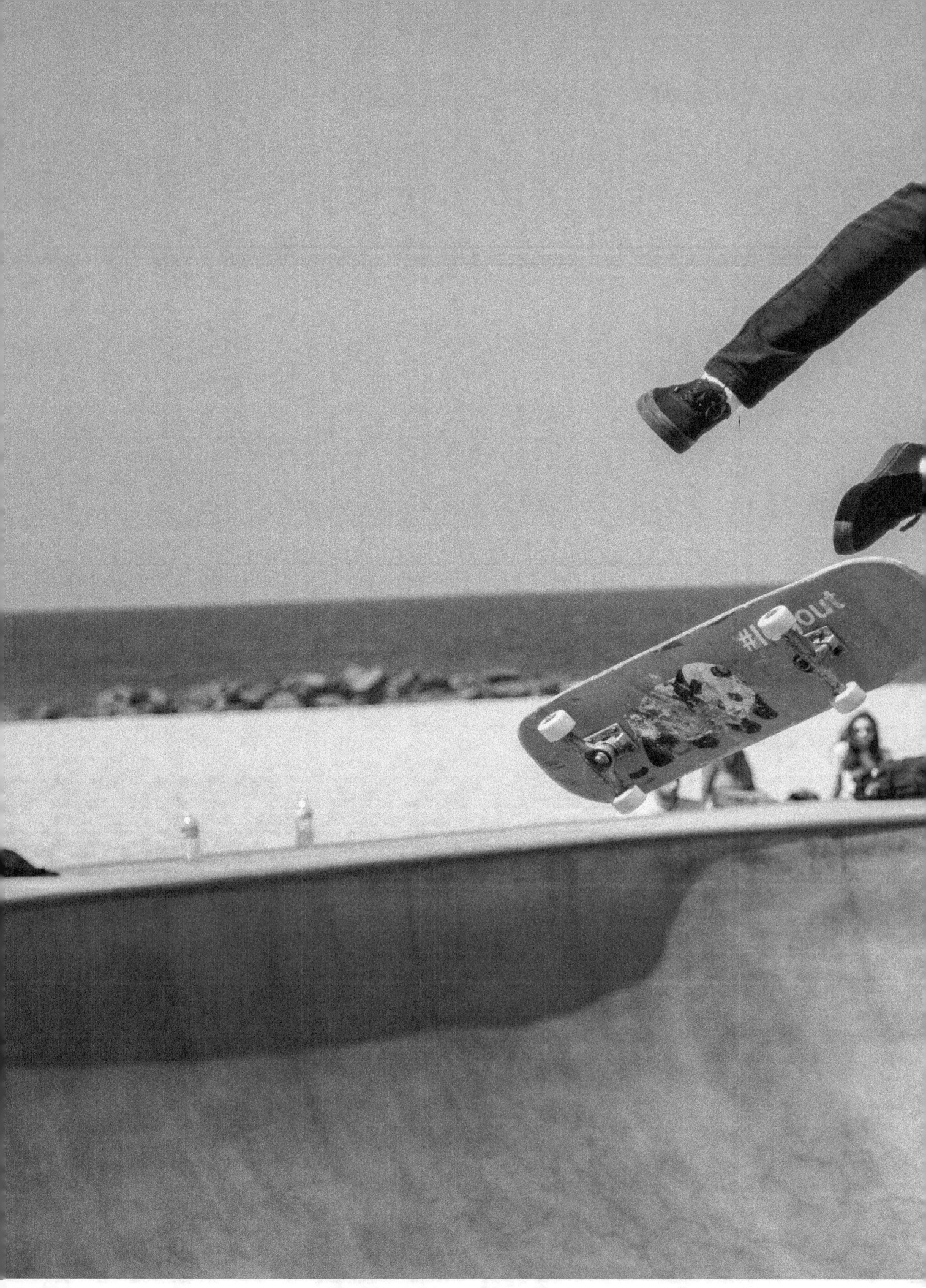

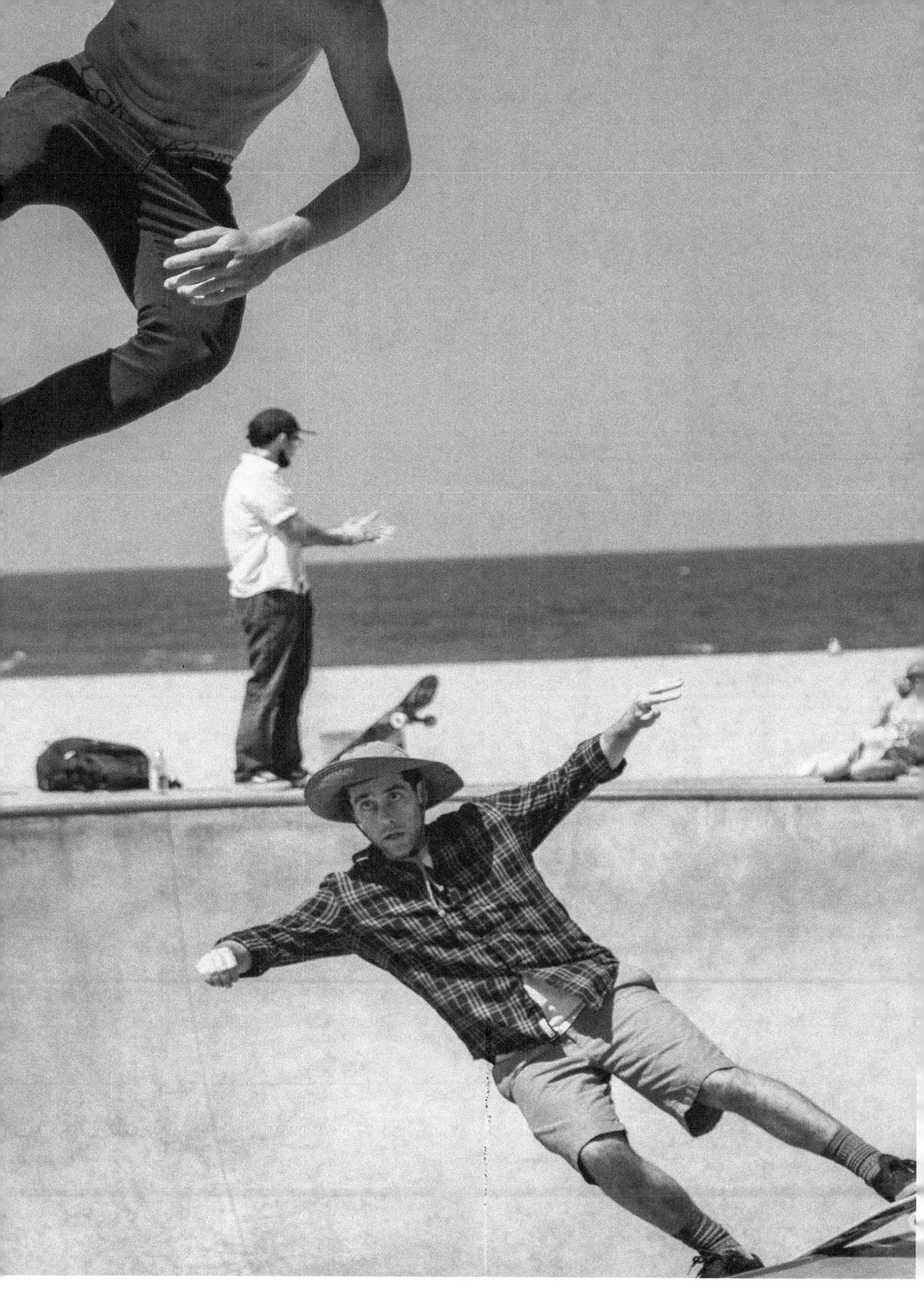

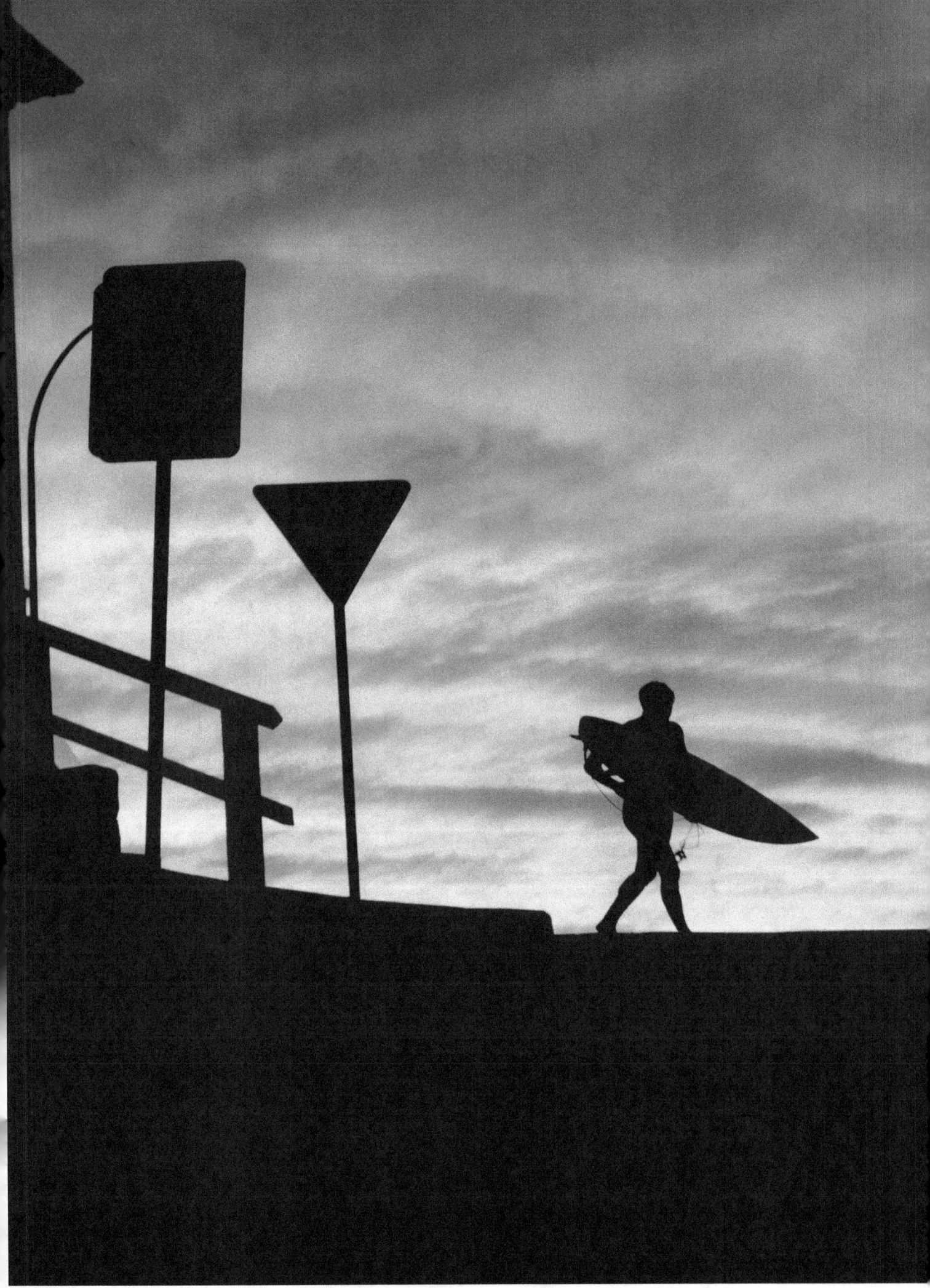

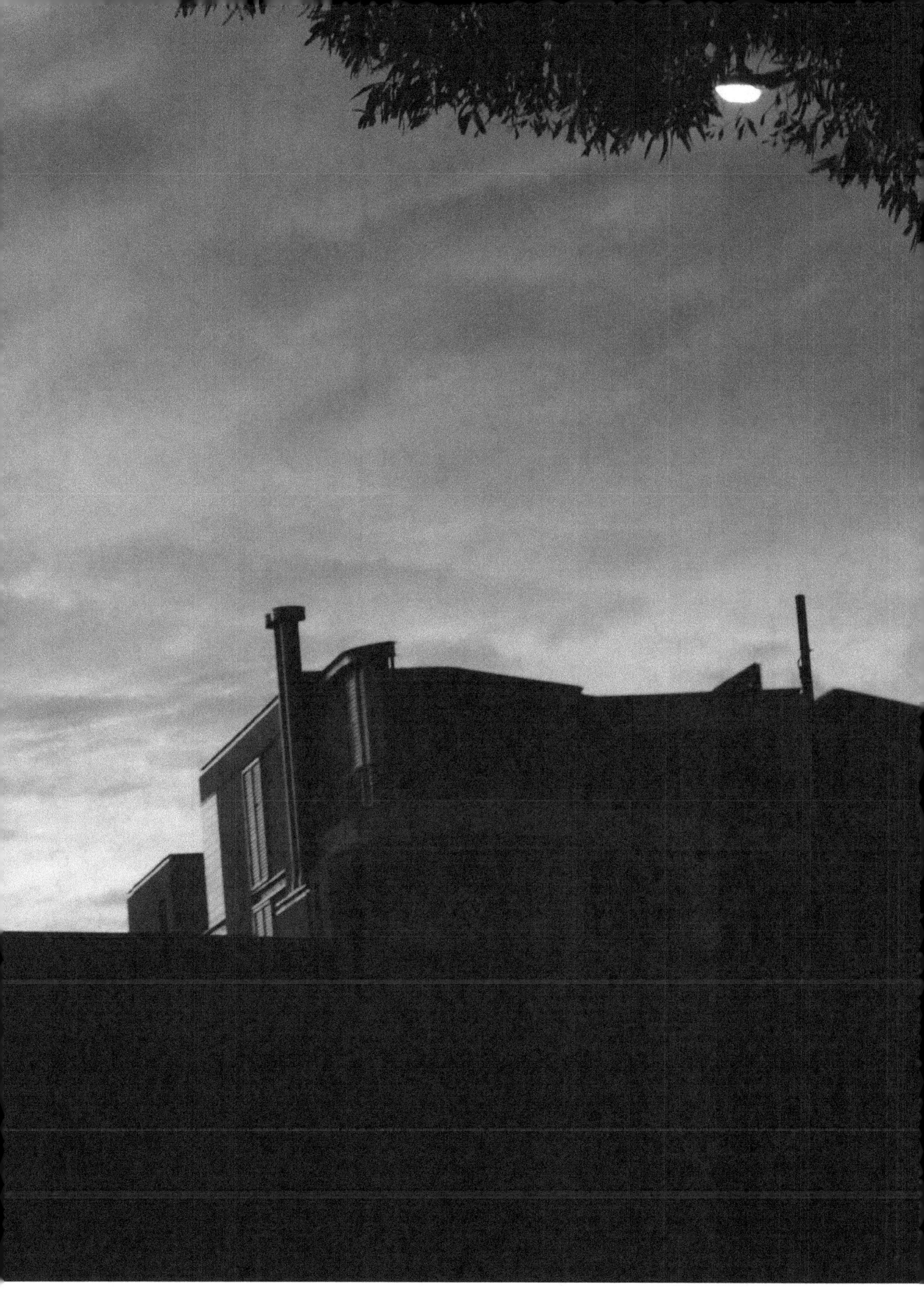

Dough Greene
"I am more myself in a garden
than anywhere else on earth."

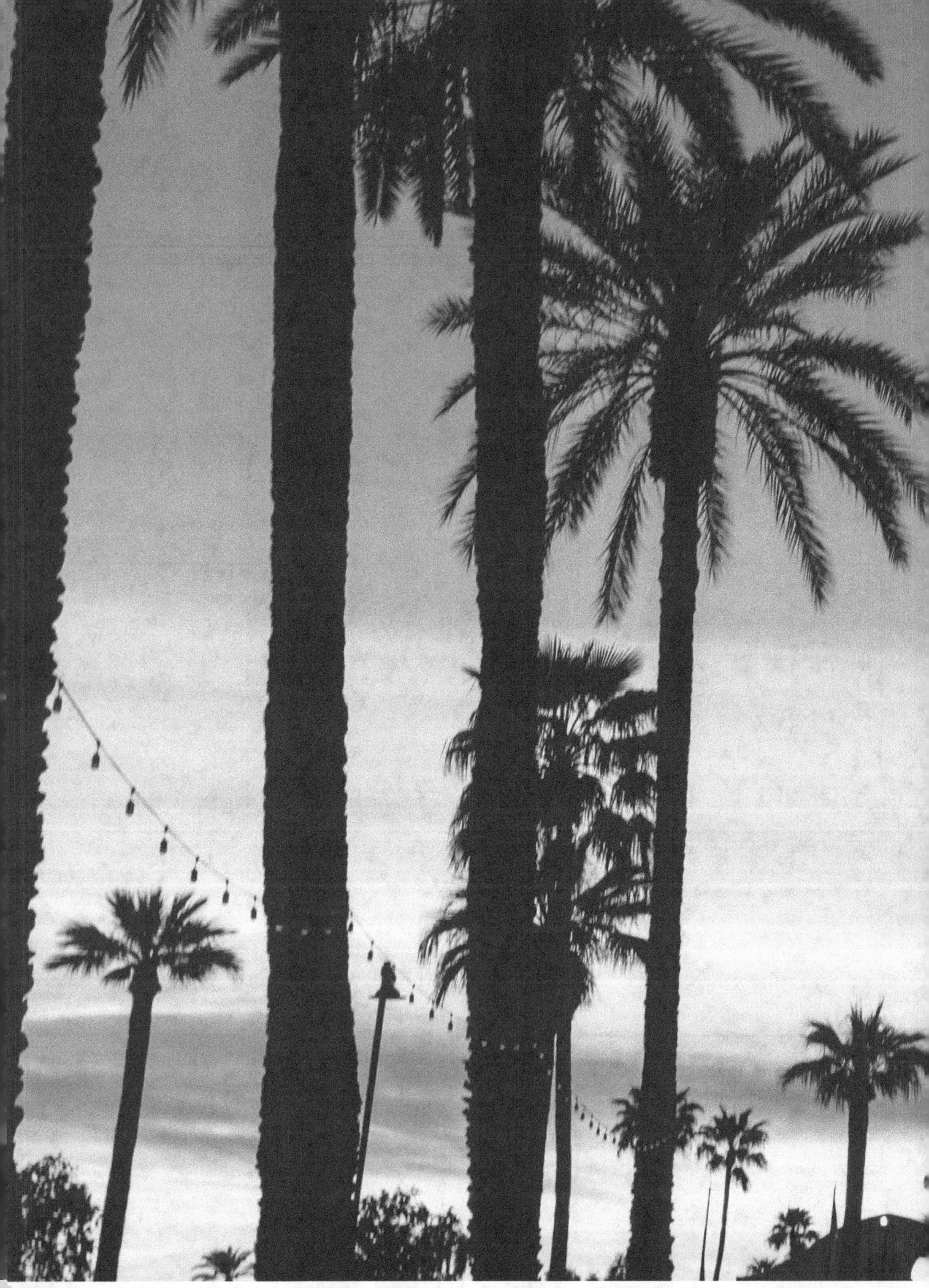

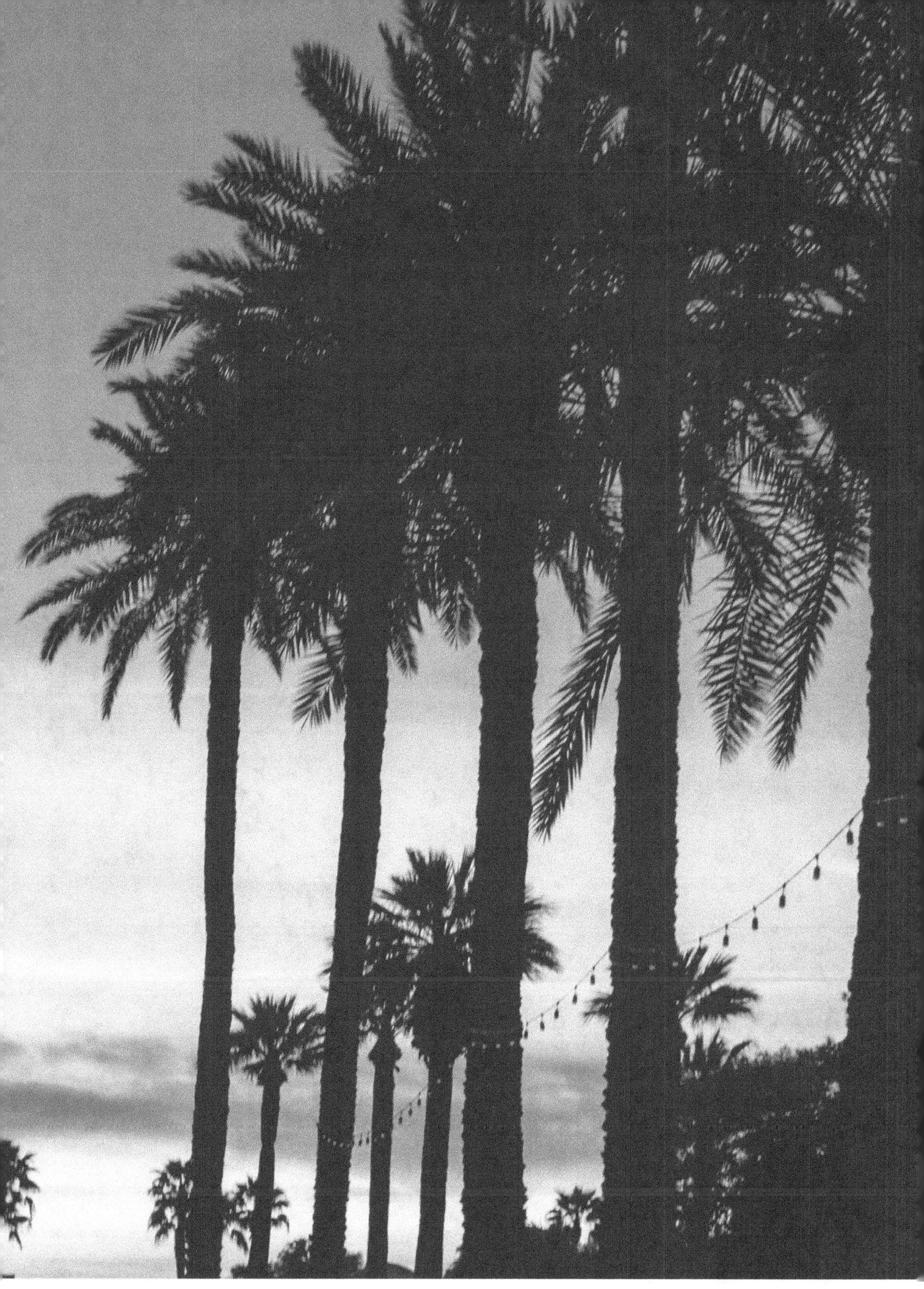

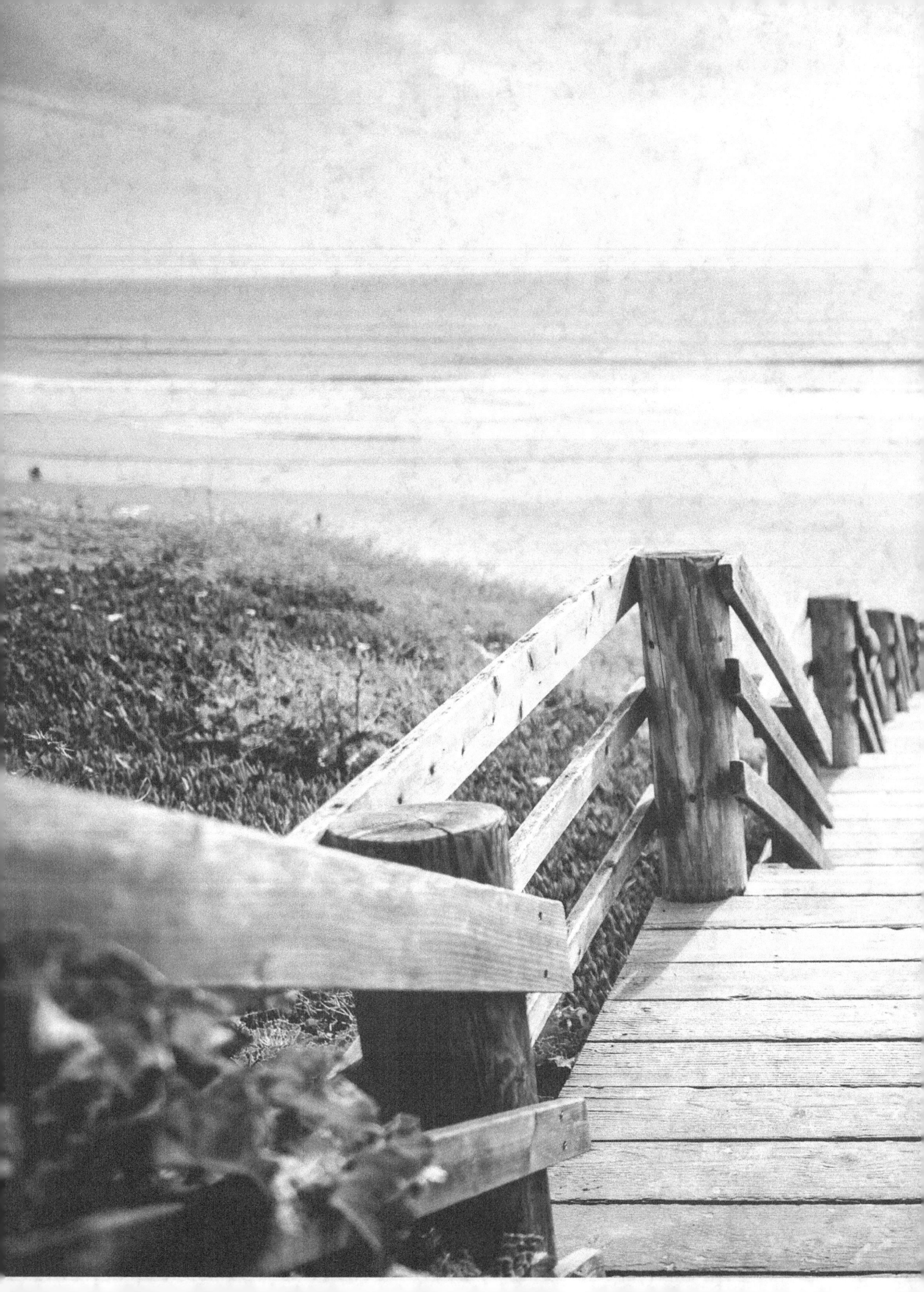

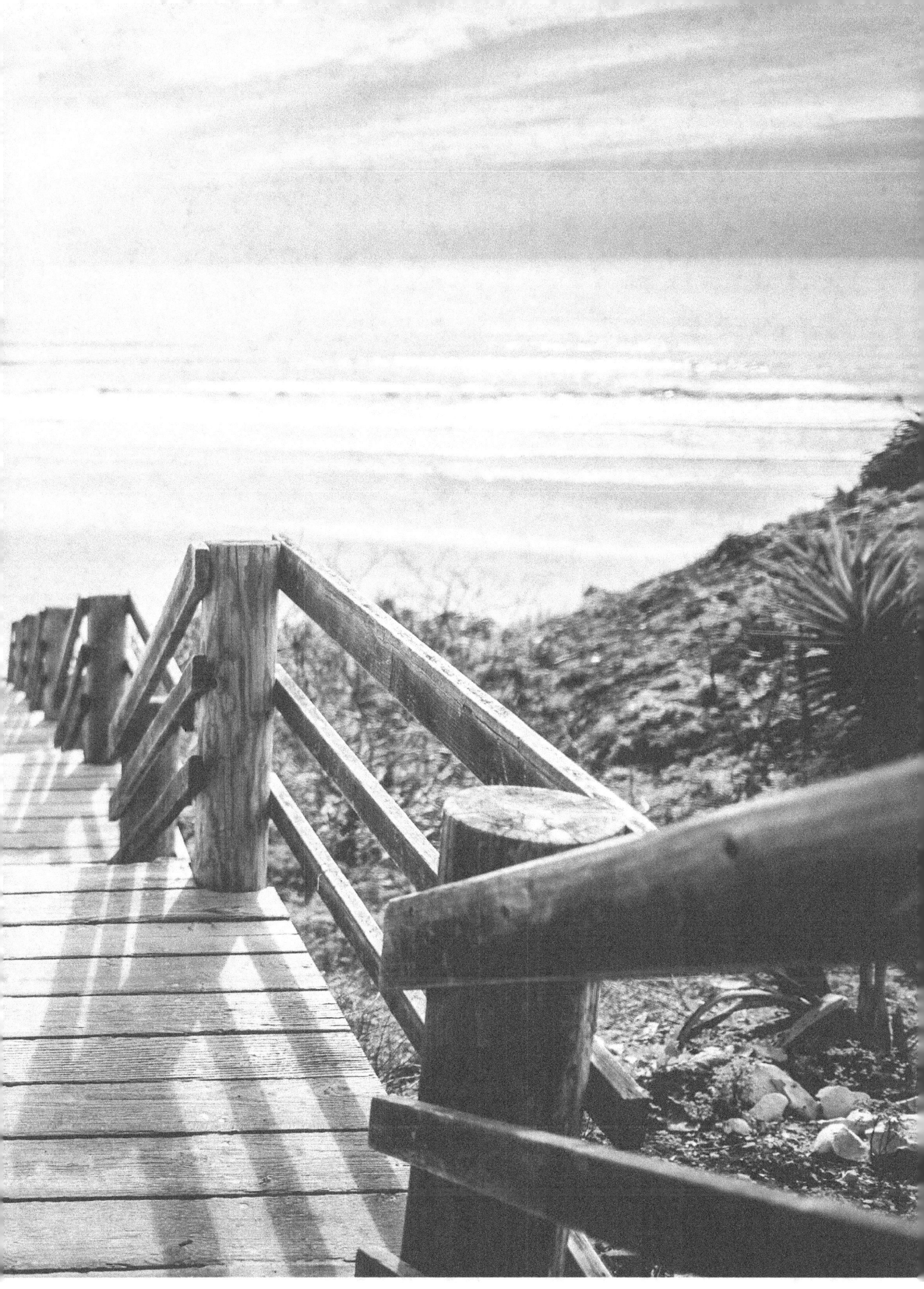

John Mayer
"'Cause a little bit of summer is what the whole year is all about."

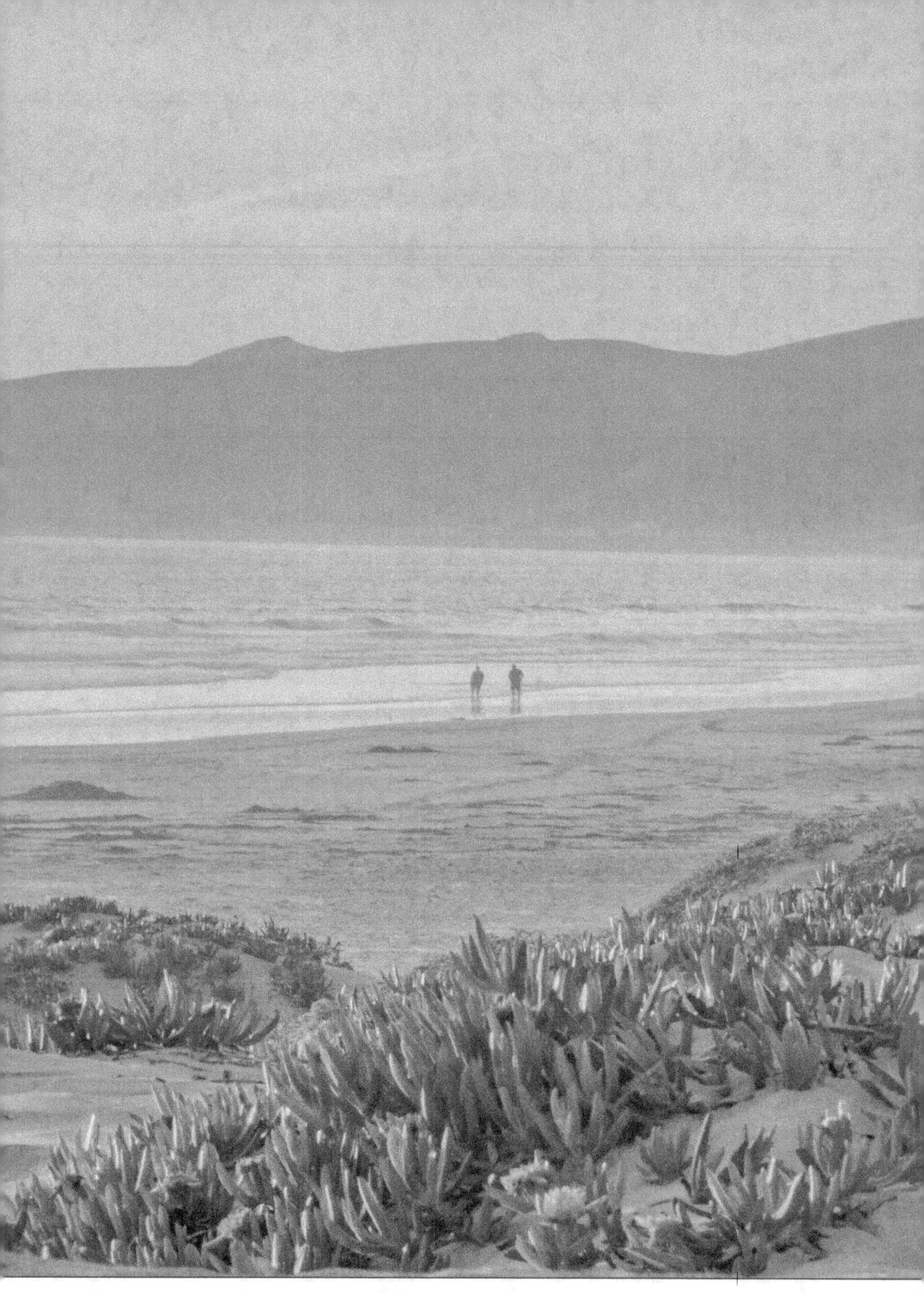

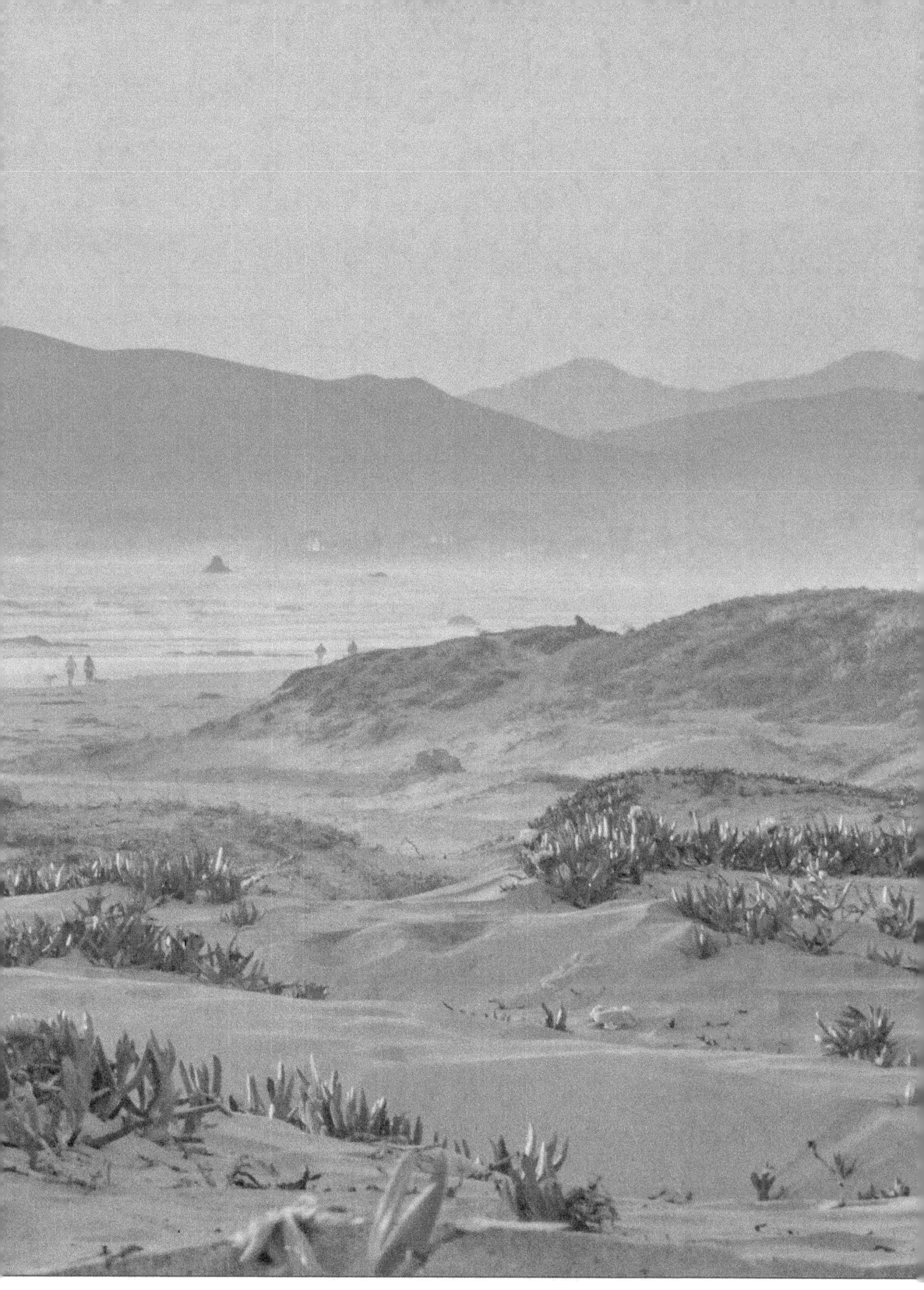

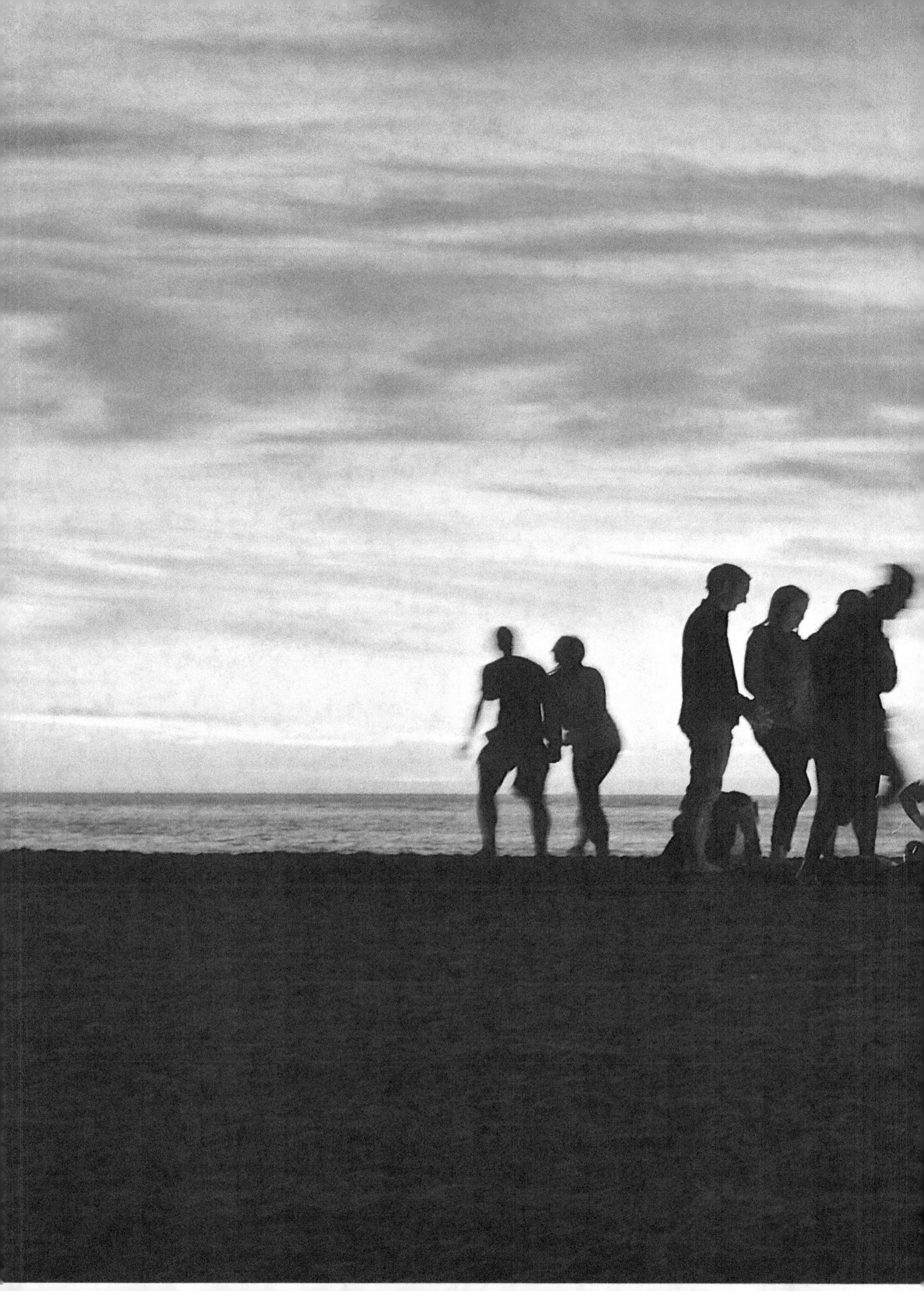

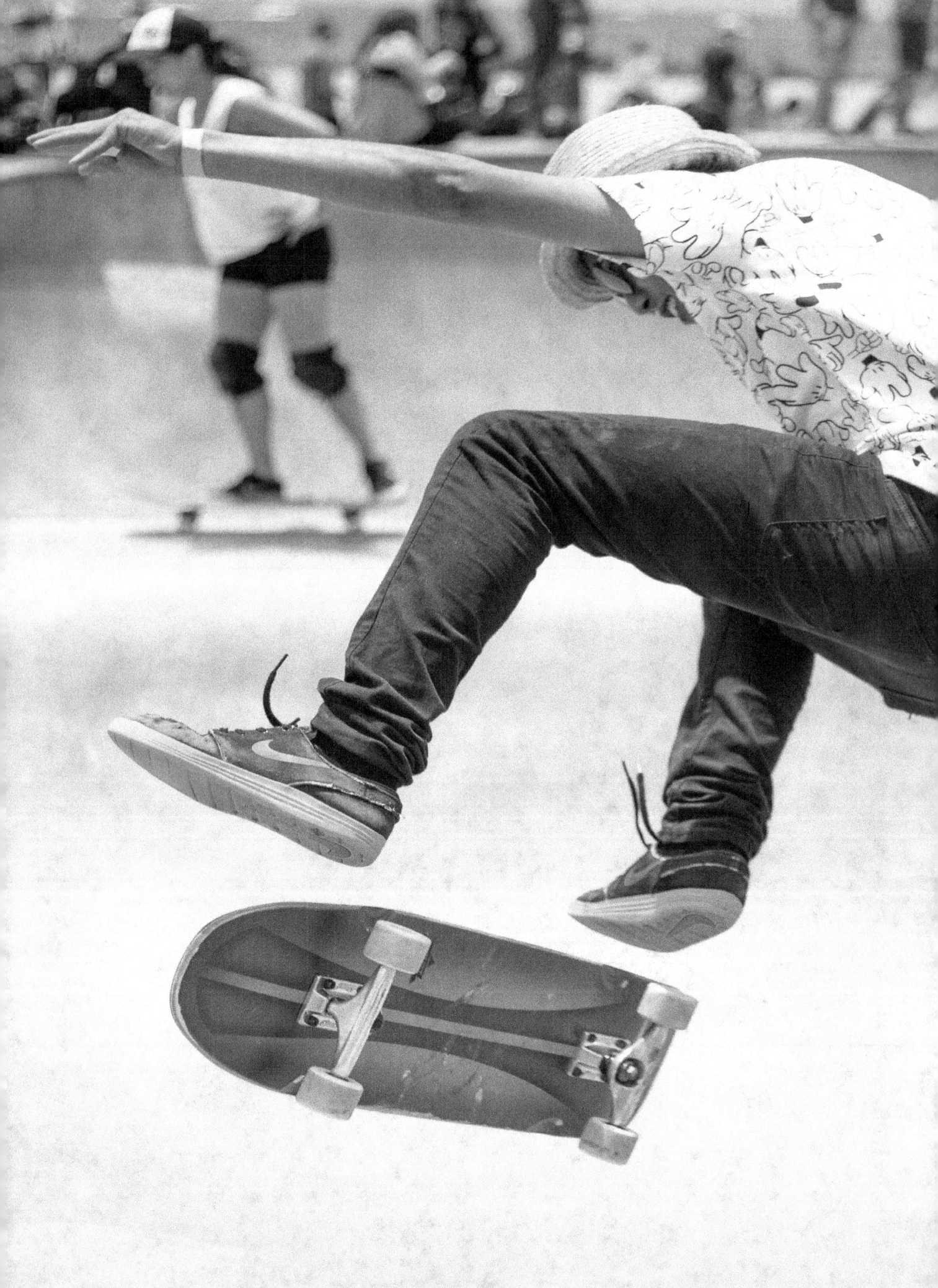

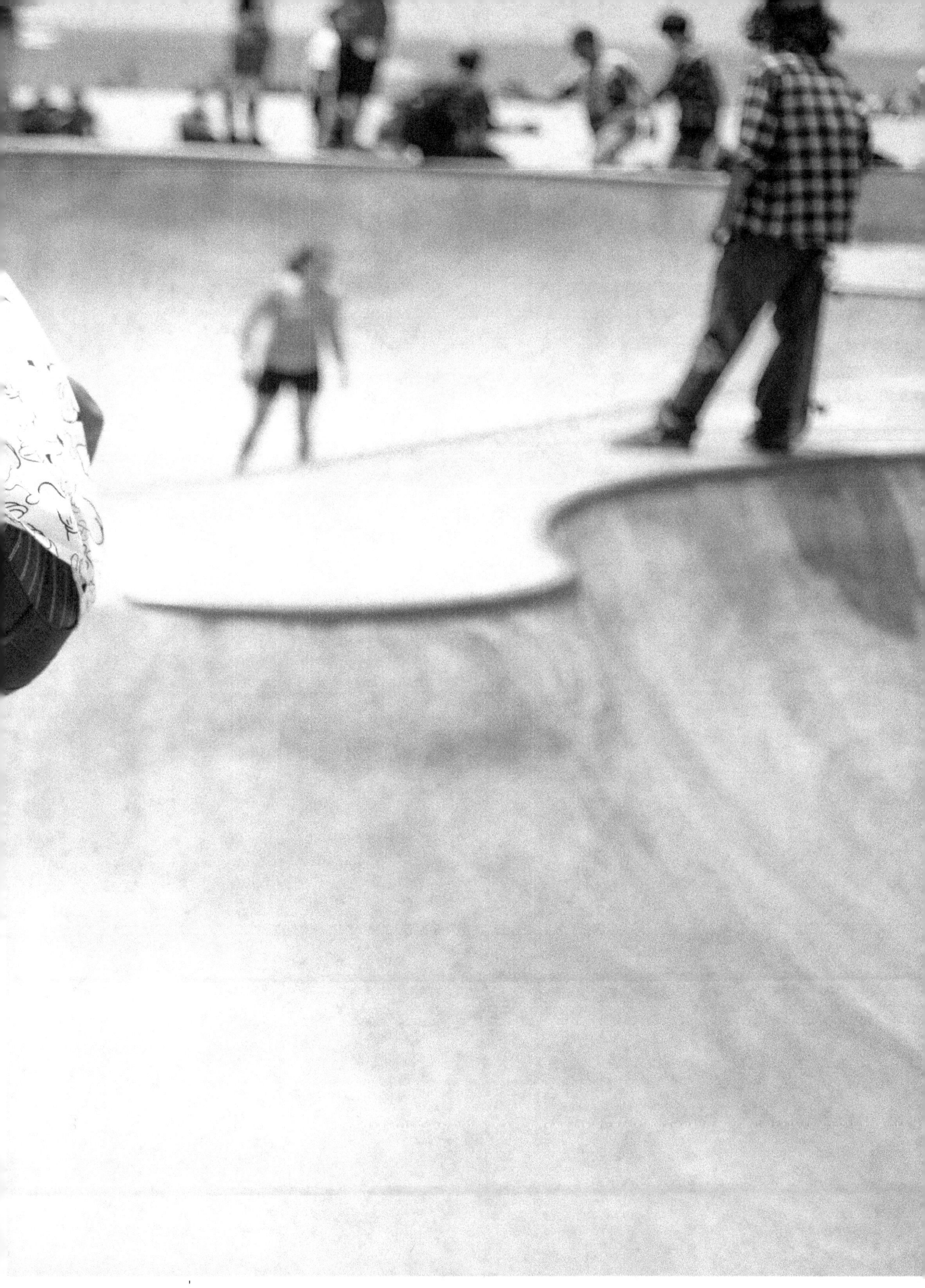

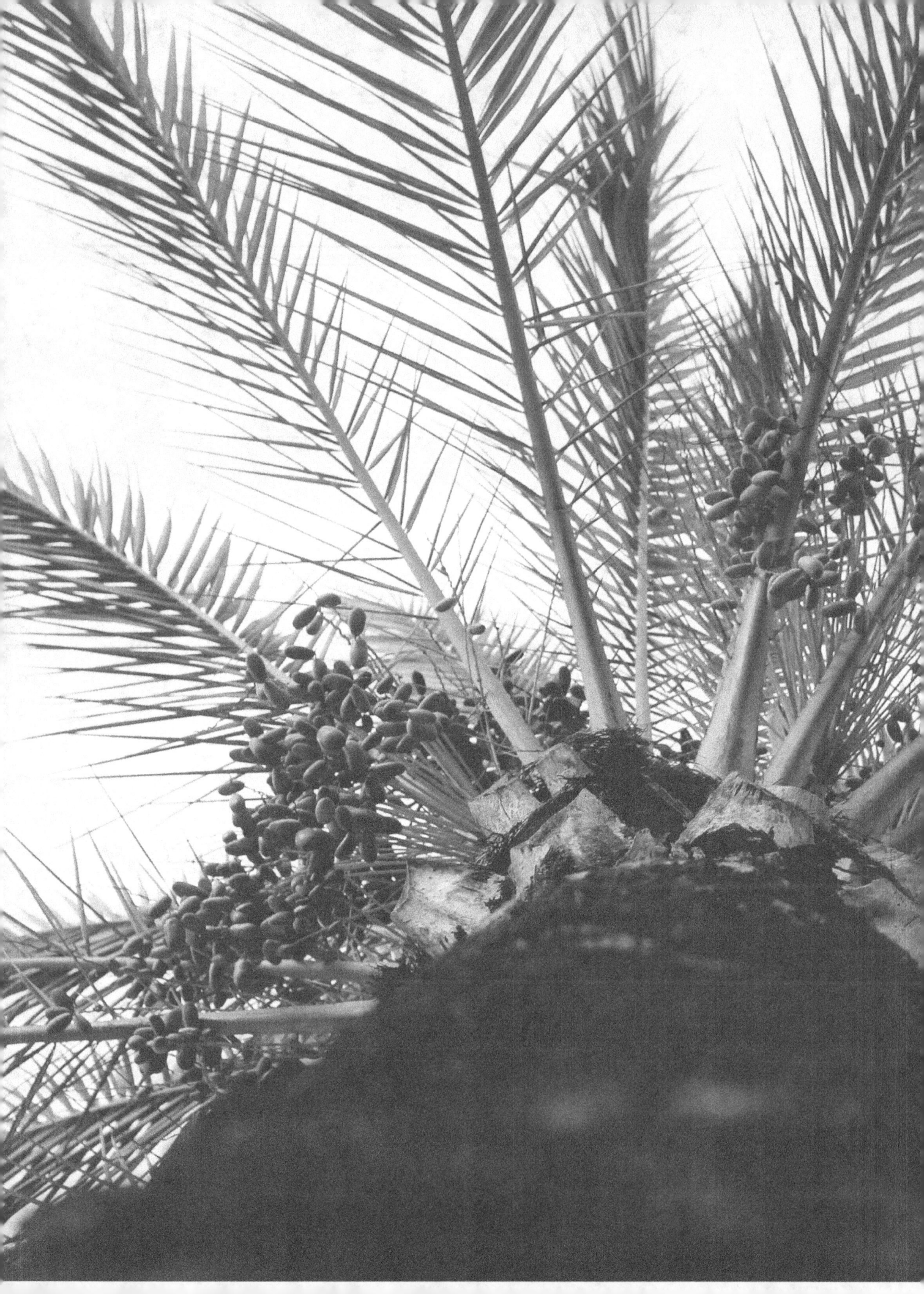

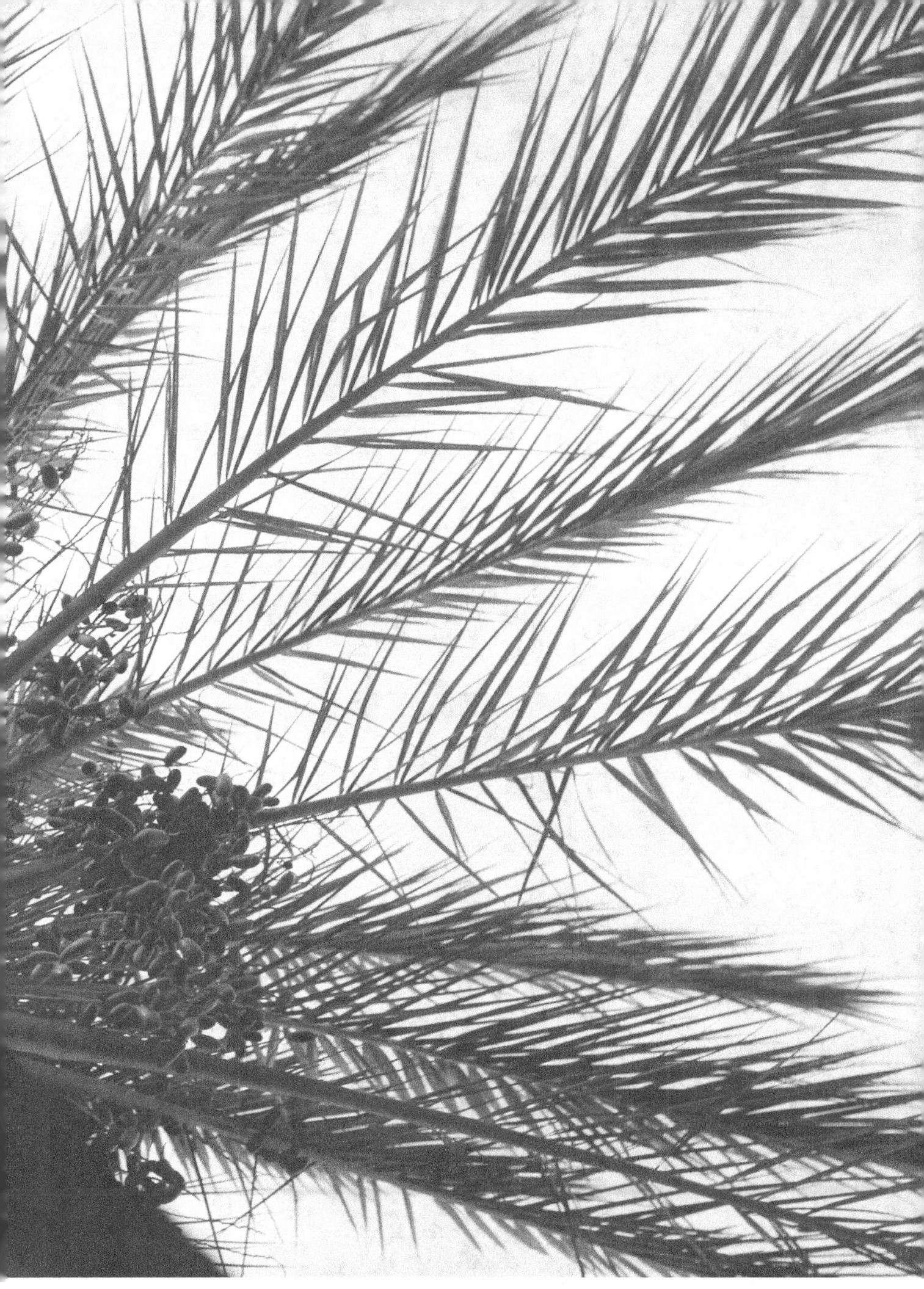

Bryan Procter
"Oh, the summer night, has a smile of light, and she sits on a sapphire throne."

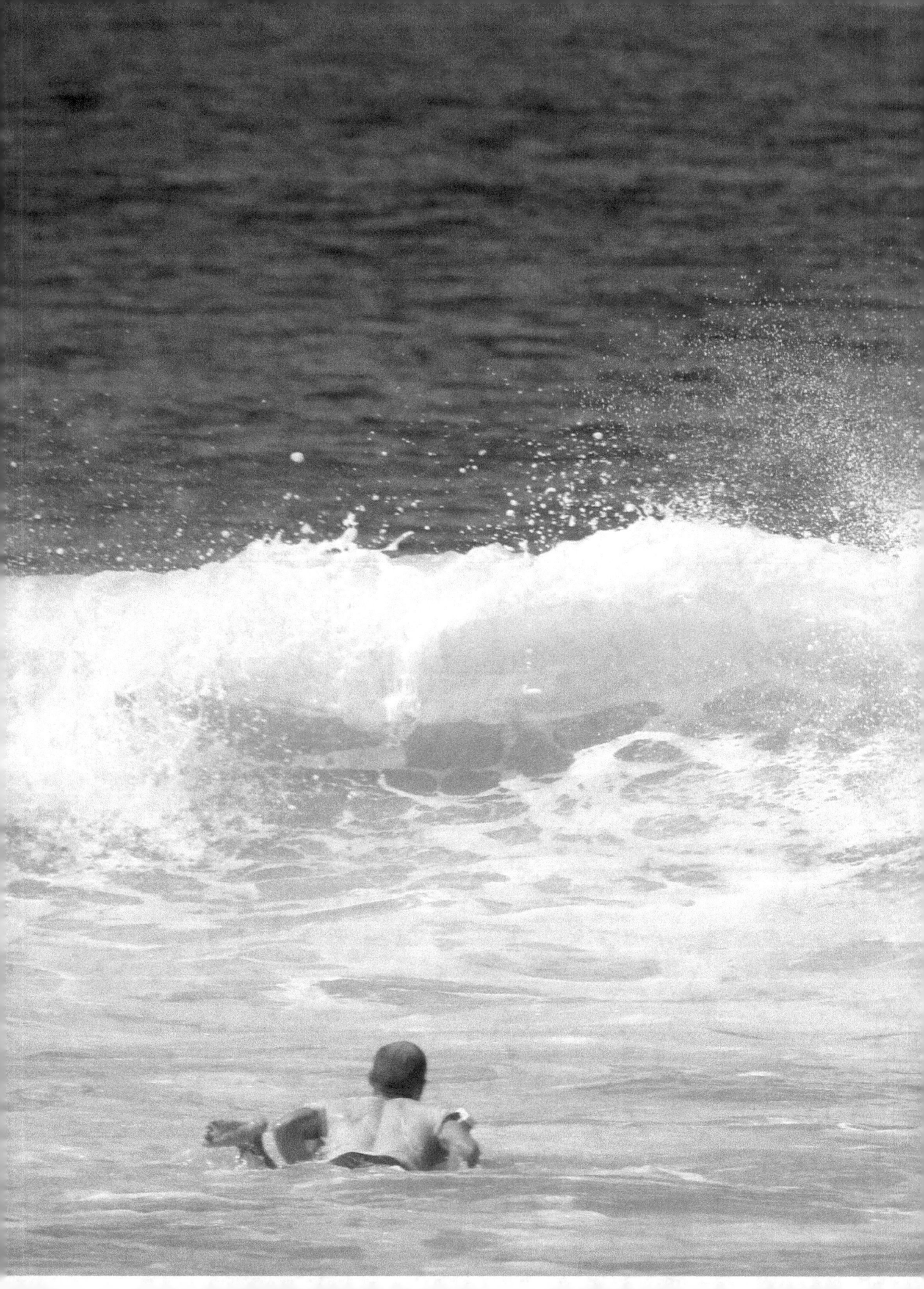

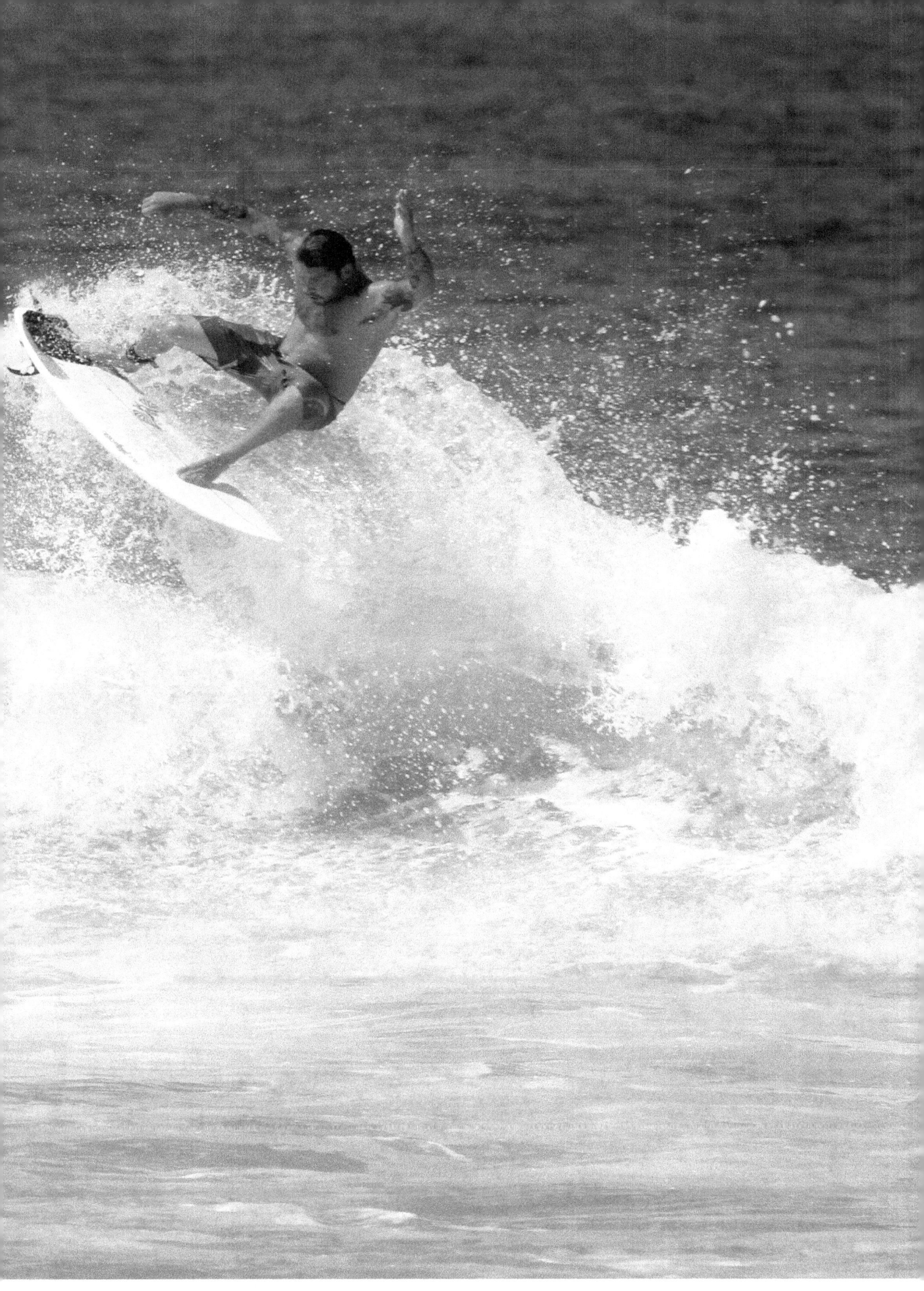

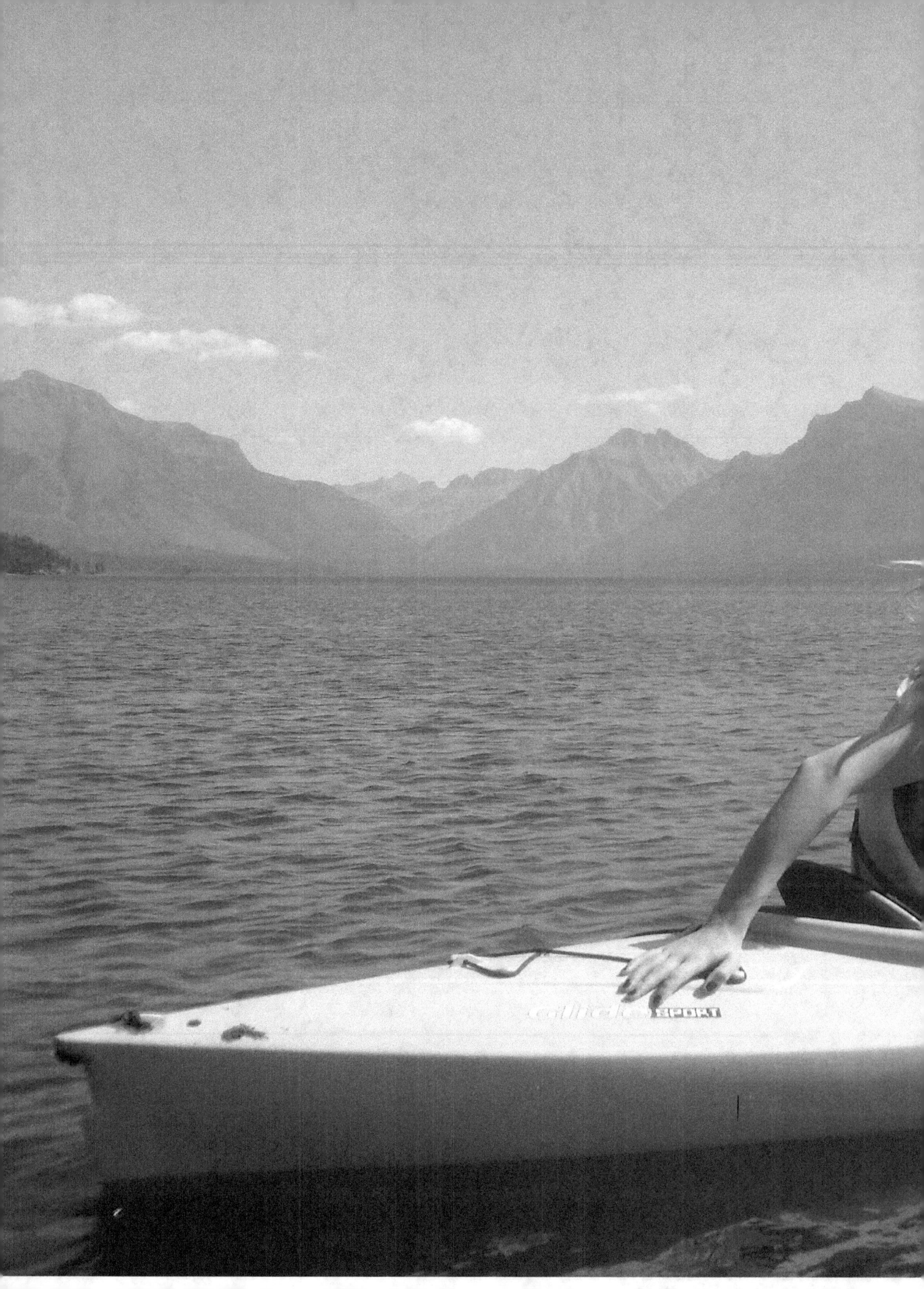

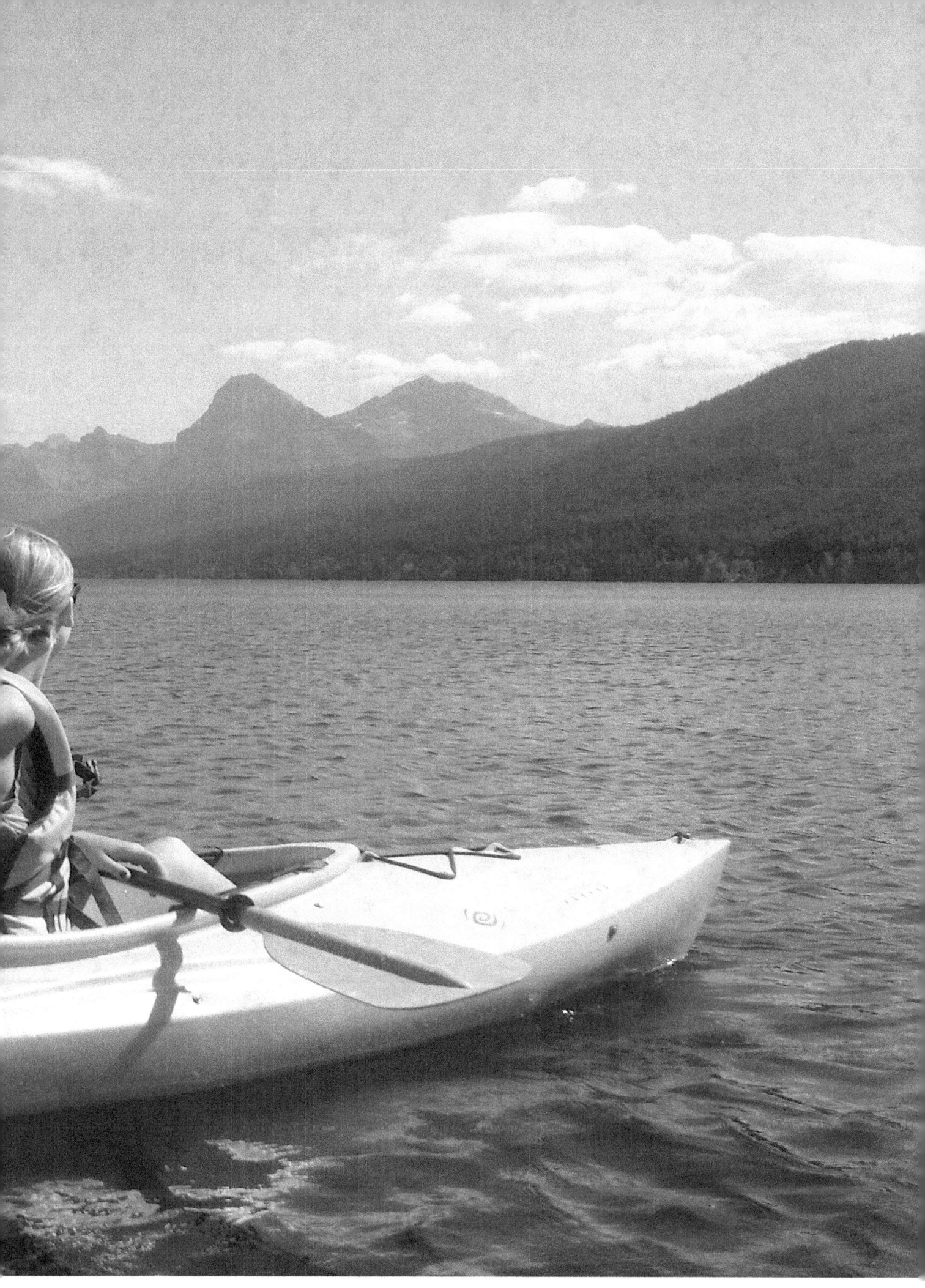

Mario Fernández
"Rise above the storm and
you will find the sunshine."

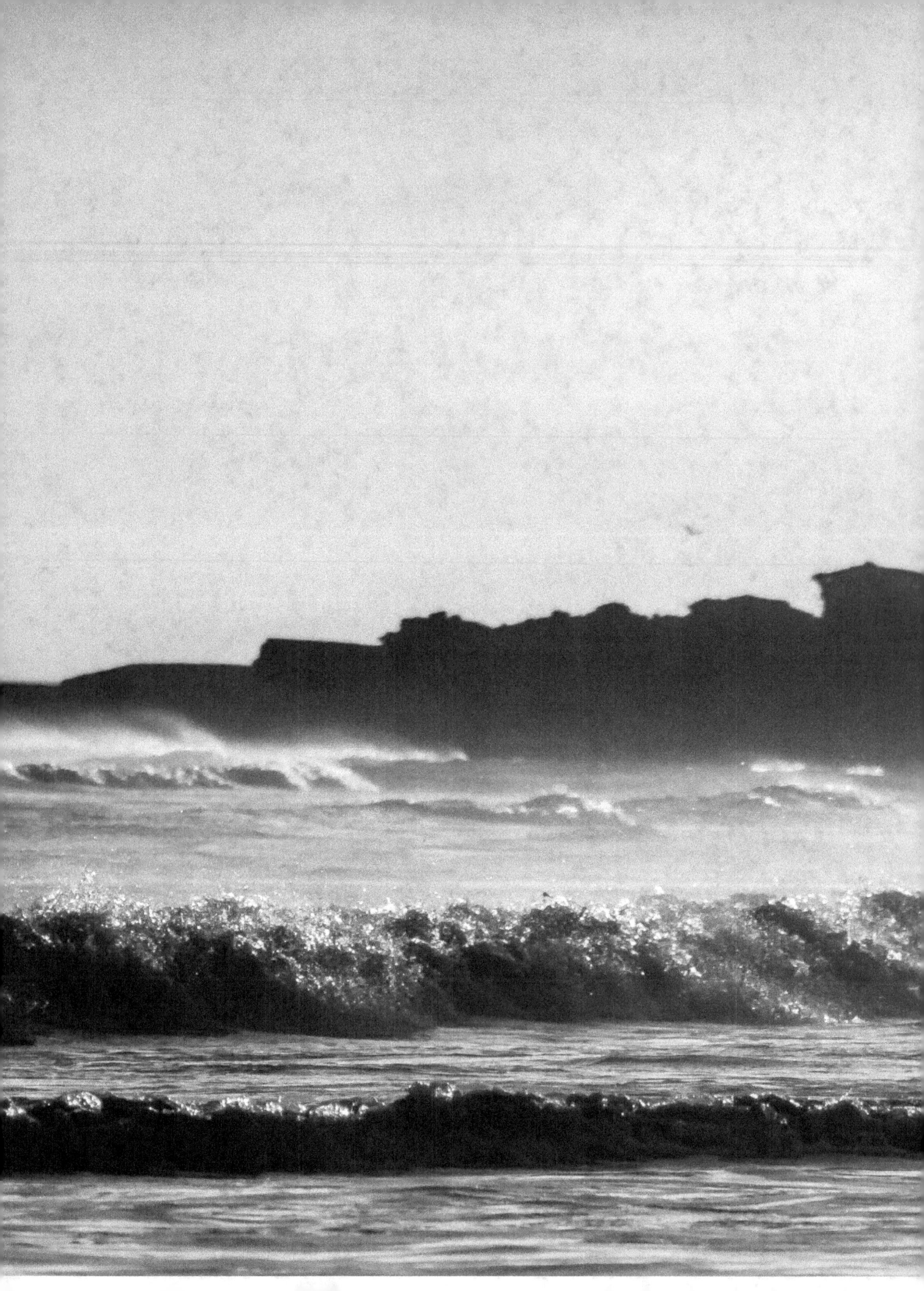

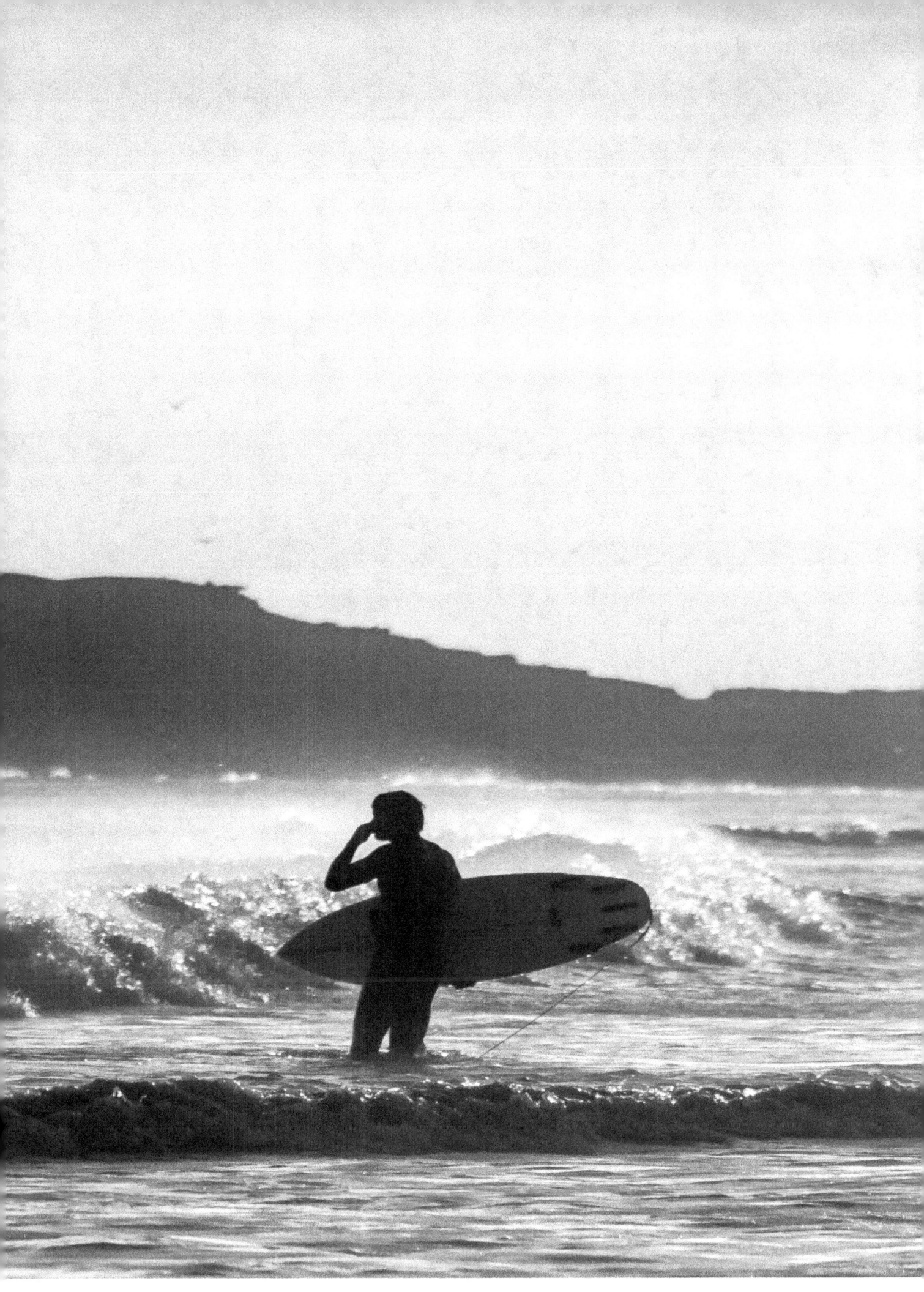

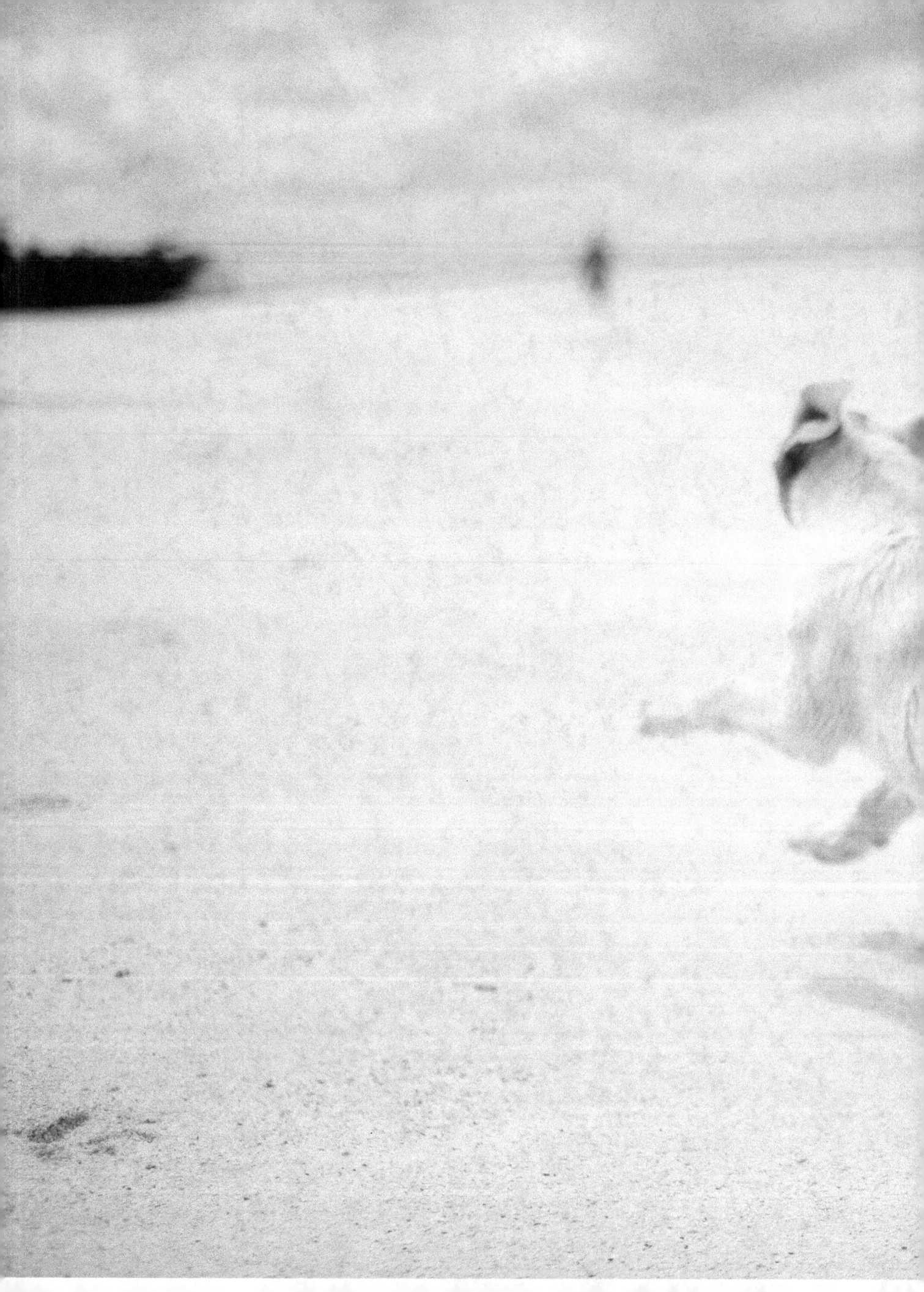

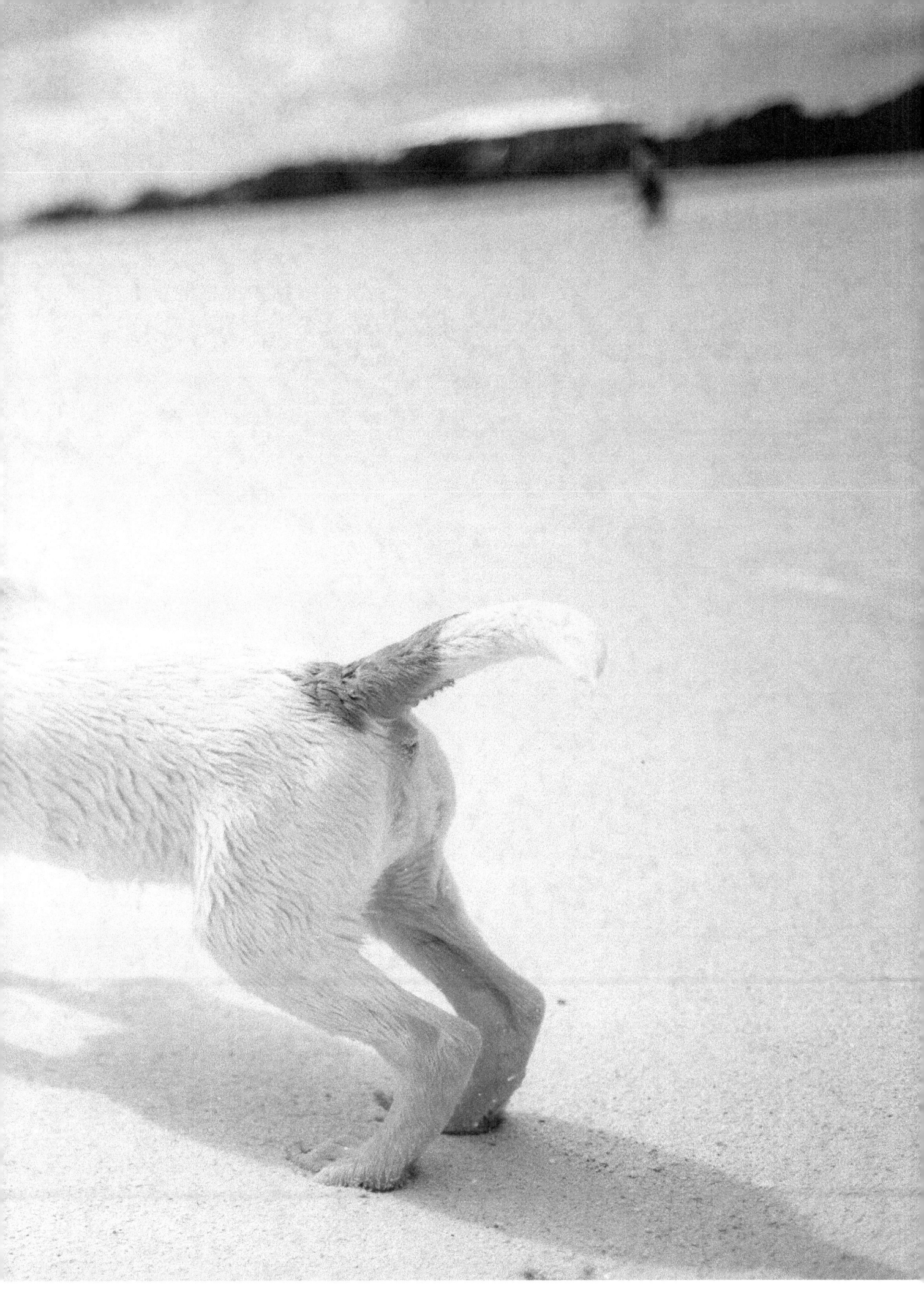

www.ingramcontent.com/pod-product-compliance
Lightning Source LLC
Chambersburg PA
CBHW081208180526
45170CB00006B/2256